Contemporary Perspectives on C.S. Lewis' *The Abolition of Man*

Also available from Bloomsbury

A Philosophical Walking Tour with C.S. Lewis, Stewart Goetz
C.S. Lewis and the Church, edited by Judith Wolfe and Brendan N. Wolfe

Contemporary Perspectives on C.S. Lewis' *The Abolition of Man*

History, Philosophy, Education, and Science

Edited by

Tim Mosteller and Gayne John Anacker

BLOOMSBURY ACADEMIC
LONDON • NEW YORK • OXFORD • NEW DELHI • SYDNEY

BLOOMSBURY ACADEMIC
Bloomsbury Publishing Plc
50 Bedford Square, London, WC1B 3DP, UK
1385 Broadway, New York, NY 10018, USA

BLOOMSBURY, BLOOMSBURY ACADEMIC and the Diana logo are
trademarks of Bloomsbury Publishing Plc

First published in Great Britain 2017
Paperback edition first published 2018

A catalogue record for this book is available from the British Library.

Library of Congress Cataloging-in-Publication Data
Names: Mosteller, Timothy, editor. | Anacker, Gayne, editor.
Title: Contemporary perspectives on C.S. Lewis' Abolition of man : history,
philosophy, education, and science / edited by Tim Mosteller and Gayne
Anacker.
Description: London ; New York : Bloomsbury Academic, 2017. | Includes
bibliographical references and index.
Identifiers: LCCN 2016039279 (print) | LCCN 2016056898 (ebook) |
ISBN 9781474296441 (hardback) | ISBN 9781474296472 (ePDF) | ISBN 9781474296458 (ePub)
Subjects: LCSH: Lewis, C. S. (Clive Staples), 1898-1963. Abolition of man. |
Civilization, Western–Philosophy. | Civilization,
Modern–1950–-Philosophy. | Natural law. | Education–Philosophy. |
Theological anthropology–Christianity. | BISAC: PHILOSOPHY / Criticism.
Classification: LCC CB245 .C66 2017 (print) | LCC CB245 (ebook) | DDC
909/.09821–dc23LC record available at https://lccn.loc.gov/2016039279

ISBN: HB: 978-1-4742-9644-1
PB: 978-1-3500-8223-6
ePDF: 978-1-4742-9647-2
ePub: 978-1-4742-9645-8

Typeset by RefineCatch Limited, Bungay, Suffolk

To find out more about our authors and books visit
www.bloomsbury.com and sign up for our newsletters.

To Adiel Brasov, in friendship—T.M.

Contents

Introduction

Tim Mosteller
California Baptist University

The purpose of this book

While I have been a fan of C.S. Lewis since my childhood, I have been teaching C.S. Lewis' *The Abolition of Man* regularly in my undergraduate philosophy courses, both at the introductory and advanced levels for nearly twenty years. While I make no claims to being a C.S. Lewis scholar, it seems reasonable to me to say that *The Abolition of Man* is very different from Lewis' other works in the following ways: its level of difficulty, its logical rigor, its breadth of analysis, and its prescience. Perhaps it is the first of these differences from Lewis' other works that has created a lacuna in the literature of C.S. Lewis scholarship regarding *The Abolition of Man*. One would hope that after seventy-five years since its initial publication, *some* book-length treatment would be available to guide students through the text as well as to provide critical scholarship in order to advance the ideas contained in it. My co-editor, Gayne Anacker and I hope that *Contemporary Perspectives on C.S. Lewis' The Abolition of Man* will do just that.

Our book presents critical scholarship and appraisal of C.S. Lewis' seminal lectures for the 75th anniversary of their presentation. The book has five main features that we hope will help readers further their knowledge of Lewis' work. First, the book is inter-disciplinary. It consists of scholars across academic disciplines offering an assessment and elaboration of the central ideas in *The Abolition of Man*. Each chapter focuses on the major areas of thought which are raised in the lectures, including: philosophy, natural law, education, literature, politics, theology, science, biotechnology, and the connection between *The Abolition of Man* and Lewis' Ransom Trilogy, especially *That Hideous Strength*.

Second, the book answers important questions about *The Abolition of Man*, such as: Is it a "conservative" book? Is Lewis hostile to scientific inquiry? Does Lewis provide an adequate rational defense of natural moral law? Is the abolition of man imminent? Third, this book is unique. There have been no multi-authored studies on *The Abolition of Man* since its publication in the last century. Fourth, the chapters in this book are readable. While the authors of this book are top-notch scholars, the purpose of this book, while scholarly, is designed to teach readers about *The Abolition of Man*. We hope that this book will help non-experts interested in *The Abolition of Man* further their knowledge and understanding of the text.

Fifth, although this book examines Lewis' work critically, each chapter seeks to criticize *The Abolition of Man* from "within" the spirit of Lewis' work and not wholly outside of it. In *The Abolition of Man*, Lewis claims that it is possible to make advances in moral knowledge by critical means, but there are two types of criticism by means of which such advances can be attempted. The first is "within" the spirit of the reality of objective value (what Lewis calls the *Tao*) by those who see that objective value is real. The second is "without" or external to the reality of objective value. Lewis accepts the first way, and rejects the second. The authors of this book also accept the first way and reject the second with regard to our attempt to advance knowledge both of *The Abolition of Man* and also our knowledge of the moral realities (including, but not limited to, politics, law, theology, science, technology, education) that Lewis deals with in *The Abolition of Man*. We are working within the objectivity of value, and not without it, because we believe that Lewis was right about this idea. As his students, we hope that we have been faithful to our master, as Lewis was to his.

Chapter summaries

Chapter 1 begins with an overview of the philosophical views presented by Lewis in *The Abolition of Man*. Adam C. Pesler (US Air Force Academy) focuses on the role of emotions in moral knowledge which is so central to

Lewis' argument right from the beginning of his lectures. The place of subjectivism and its attendant problems are also considered.

Chapter 2 considers the role in which the concept of natural law functions in Lewis' understanding of the doctrine of objective value. Micah Watson (Calvin College) explains the way in which Lewis defends the use of reason and the ways in which it can be corrupted, and its proper end. This chapter also explores the place of Lewis' understanding of natural law in the broader study of natural moral law.

In Chapter 3 Mark Pike (University of Leeds) considers what *The Abolition of Man* teaches us about education. Since Lewis makes it very clear in the subtitle of the text that his lectures are reflections on education, this chapter will assist us in our understanding of how education ought to be approached if Lewis' arguments in *The Abolition of Man* are themselves persuasive. Professor Pike focuses on the specific task that Lewis undertakes in the teaching of moral education, providing insight into this key function of education as such.

Chapter 4 by Charlie W. Starr (Independent Scholar) considers how the teaching of English is informed by the ideas in *The Abolition of Man*. Again, the subtitle of the lectures is not just on teaching and education, but on the teaching of the particular subject of the English language. This chapter shows how Lewis begins his lectures with an example from his own discipline considers the crucial ideas surrounding the objectivity of value, and leads us to a clear understanding of how English should be taught.

Chapter 5 takes up the question of politics and conservatism in *The Abolition of Man*. As Francis J. Beckwith (Baylor University) points out, *The Abolition of Man* has been hailed by conservative thinkers as one of the most important conservative political offerings of the twentieth century. Beckwith considers the question of whether Lewis' lectures are in fact conservative. Beckwith places this question squarely within considerations of Lewis' views in light of contemporary legal and moral issues and distinguishes ways in which the concept of conservatism can be applied to Lewis' work.

While Lewis' *The Abolition of Man* is not a theological treatise, Lewis makes it explicit that he believes that the way in which we approach the idea of objective value will have crucial implications for theology (as well as ethics and politics). In Chapter 6, Judith Wolfe (University of St. Andrews) explores the way in which Lewis' idea of natural law is underpinned by theology and the ways in which this text is "Merely Christian."

Chapter 7 considers Lewis' view of science. David Ussery (Arkansas Center for Genomic and Ecological Medicine, University of Arkansas Medical School) gives us a working scientist's perspective on *The Abolition of Man*. Ussery shows how Lewis' ideas regarding the objectivity of value can influence a scientist's perspective on the relation of science to other disciplines (e.g., ethics), but Ussery also argues that Lewis' views can give us insight into science as such.

In Chapter 8, James A. Herrick (Hope College) takes a look at the major ideas of Lewis' day that were behind Lewis' need to offer a defense of the objectivity of value, particularly the work of J.D. Bernal, J.B.S. Haldane, and Olaf Stapledon. Herrick considers how Lewis understood the ideas of these thinkers if taken seriously and implemented without question constituted a clear threat to our humanity and to humanity itself.

Chapter 9 concludes with an analysis of the relationship between *The Abolition of Man* and *That Hideous Strength*, which Lewis claims to contain the same concepts but in a different genre of writing. Scott B. Key (California Baptist University) shows how the main characters, Mark and Jane Studdock, and their interaction with the major forces in *That Hideous Strength*, exemplify in a literary way the philosophical concepts argued for in *The Abolition of Man*. While *The Abolition of Man* can appear to end on a negative note, Key shows how Lewis sees the possibility of redemption even in a world that has largely rejected the objectivity of value.

1

Philosophy in *The Abolition of Man*

Adam C. Pelser
US Air Force Academy

G.K. Chesterton once wrote that

> Philosophy is merely thought that has been thought out. It is often a great bore. But man has no alternative, except between being influenced by thought that has been thought out and being influenced by thought that has not been thought out. The latter is what we commonly call culture and enlightenment today.
>
> 1950, p. 176

While Chesterton is right that too many people are influenced by unphilosophical "thought that has not been thought out"—harmful gifts often concealed in the shiny wrapping of "cool" catchphrases and savvy slogans—the mere fact that a thought has been thought out is no guarantee that it is true. While philosophy can help us to avoid certain errors of sloppy and uncritical thinking, not all thought that has been thought out has been thought out well. Not all philosophy is good philosophy.

Though not a professor of philosophy himself, C.S. Lewis understood the intellectual and cultural significance of philosophy, often better than his colleagues in philosophy departments, and he regularly engaged with the influential philosophers and philosophies of his day in his writing and in public debates. As a Fellow of Magdalen College, Oxford, where he was a tutor of English Language and Literature, Lewis held keys to the ivory tower of academia (indeed, he quite literally had access to the iron key to Magdalen Tower, the tallest building in Oxford). Rather than locking his erudition away in the ivory tower, however, Lewis focused much of his work on counteracting the influence of bad academic philosophy on the thinking of the common (that is not to say unintelligent or uneducated) people outside the walls of academia. Lewis had the rare ability to engage with the popular philosophies of his day, both as they were expressed by their philosophical proponents and as they were propounded by "enlightened" culture-shapers, often uncritically in the form of "thought that had not been thought out."

As a case in point, C.S. Lewis' triad of essays published as *The Abolition of Man* is a sustained critique of an insidious philosophical view—namely, moral subjectivism—that had come to be, and still is today, widely touted and accepted as a kind of cultural orthodoxy. The central theses of *The Abolition of Man* are that subjectivism is inherently dangerous for human society, and that subjectivists are guilty at best of ignorant inconsistency and at worst of vicious absurdity. *The Abolition of Man* is thus an attempt to help people to "think out" the consequences of subjectivism, to follow it to its logical and (frightening) practical conclusions.

I first focus on Lewis' arguments against subjectivism, which have been the subject of a good deal of scholarly attention (e.g., Kreeft, 1994; Elshtain, 2008). What is often missed, or underemphasized, by casual readers of *The Abolition of Man* and Lewis scholars alike, however, is the positive role emotions play in Lewis' alternative account of moral knowledge. The importance of emotions for knowledge of objective value (moral and otherwise) will be my second focus. Finally, I will follow Lewis in contrasting two different approaches to moral (emotional) education—character cultivation and conditioning—in an attempt to help chart a course, or, rather, rediscover an ancient course away from the island of the abolition of man to which the Sirens of subjectivism beckon.*

Beware the Sirens of subjectivism

Lewis begins his essay "Men Without Chests" by introducing the reader to an English textbook for elementary school students, which Lewis calls *The Green Book*. In *The Green Book* the authors, whom Lewis refers to as Gaius and Titius, discuss a story in which one tourist calls a waterfall "sublime" and another

* Some material in the following two sections is adapted with permission from Pelser (2014).

tourist calls it "pretty," and Coleridge responds by endorsing the first judgment and vehemently rejecting the second. Lewis quotes the following passage from *The Green Book*:

> When the man said *This is sublime*, he appeared to be making a remark about the waterfall ... Actually ... he was not making a remark about the waterfall, but a remark about his own feelings. What he was saying was really *I have feelings associated in my mind with the word "Sublime"*, or shortly, *I have sublime feelings* ... This confusion is continually present in language as we use it. We appear to be saying something very important about something: and actually we are only saying something about our own feelings.
>
> 2001a, pp. 2–3

Lewis notes that, "The schoolboy who reads this passage in *The Green Book* will believe two propositions: firstly, that all sentences containing a predicate of value are statements about the emotional state of the speaker, and secondly, that all such statements are unimportant" (p. 3). Perhaps unknowingly, Gaius and Titius were promulgating a view that Lewis rightly identifies as moral "subjectivism" (p. 27). Subjectivism is the view that value claims such as "Murder is wrong," which might seem to be claims about objective (mind-independent) values, are simply reports about the subjective emotions of the speaker (e.g., "I have a disapproving feeling toward murder"), which are no more about objective values than statements such as "I have an itch" or "I'm going to be sick."[1]

If statements of value really amount to nothing more than reports of one's own feelings, then it will be impossible ever to say that anything has value of an objective, mind-independent sort (that is, value that a thing has whether or not anyone sees or believes that it has such value). If subjectivism is true, then we can express that an action or institution makes us feel angry or indignant (by saying it is unjust), but we cannot express that it is (objectively) unjust; we can express that a piece of art or music or natural scenery gives us a feeling of aesthetic awe (by saying it is beautiful or sublime), but not that it is (objectively) beautiful or sublime.

Understood simply as a thesis about the meaning of value claims, subjectivism is not strictly a view about the existence of objective value or about our ability to know whether a thing has objective value of one sort or another. If subjectivism is true, it might be that objective goods like justice, human wellbeing, truth, and beauty really exist and that some objects really possess and exhibit these values. We might even be able to know that they do; we just can't *say* that they do. Yet, the primary target of Lewis' second and third essays seems to be moral skepticism, not the subjectivism about moral claims in focus in "Men Without Chests." Indeed, the central thesis of "The Way" seems to be that it is at best inconsistent and at worst viciously manipulative to reject belief in the values at the heart of the natural moral law ("the *Tao*") on the basis of moral skepticism while promoting belief in other values. And the central thesis of "The Abolition of Man" seems to be that if we as a society continue to reject the possibility of moral knowledge, we will be left morally rudderless and will, in the end, become a society subject to the whims and mere appetitive urges of a small class of powerful individuals—"the Conditioners." Having lost all moral bearing, the Conditioners will engage in an unbridled quest for scientific and technological progress, ultimately succeeding in "the abolition of man" through eugenics and biotechnologies that violate the dignity of human beings and undermine their control over their own lives in service of the base and selfish desires of the few who hold power over such technologies.

Given Lewis' apparent shift in focus away from subjectivism about moral claims and toward moral skepticism, it might be objected that Lewis has confused a philosophical view about the meaning of moral language with an epistemological view about the possibility (or, rather, the impossibility) of moral knowledge. To pose such a criticism, however, would be to underestimate Lewis' philosophical sophistication. Lewis insightfully recognized that subjectivism, cutting off as it does our ability to claim that anything has objective value, is no sooner accepted as a philosophical view about moral and other value-attributing language than it gives rise to the epistemological view that we could never really know whether a thing has objective value even if it does. Subjectivism cuts off our heads from knowledge of objective value by muting our mouths and hardening our hearts. What was conceived in an ivory tower as moral subjectivism is born in the minds of modern men and women as moral skepticism. After all, what cannot be said or experienced cannot be thought. And what cannot be thought will not be believed.

Lewis' keen observation that moral subjectivism breeds moral skepticism is no less true today than it was in Lewis' day. As sociologist Christian Smith and a team of researchers recently highlighted in their book *Lost in Transition*, twenty-first-century colleges and universities are full of young adults "without chests"—that is, emotionally malformed subjectivists who believe that moral claims are nothing more than claims about the speaker's subjective emotions. As Lewis predicted, such subjectivism has led to the widespread rejection of the possibility of moral knowledge. One among the many "emerging" adults Smith and his team interviewed put it this way: "What makes something right? I mean for me I guess what makes something right is how I feel about it, but different people feel different ways, so I couldn't speak on behalf of anyone else as to what's right and what's wrong" (Smith *et al.*, 2011, p. 22). Witness the danger of *The Green Book*.

Of course, as Lewis takes pains to demonstrate, Gaius and Titius (and most others who have not sufficiently thought out their own moral subjectivism and the moral skepticism it breeds) are not prepared to give up on moral knowledge altogether. Rather, their apparent goal is to debunk certain traditional or "sentimental" values in favor of other more respectable values that happened to be in vogue among the "enlightened" men and women of the day.[2] As Lewis explains, "Their skepticism about values is on the surface: it is for use on other people's values; about the values current in their own set they are not nearly skeptical enough" (2001a, p. 29). In other words, the moral subjectivism and moral skepticism of Gaius and Titius (and that of the innocent and unsuspecting pupils whose views are formed by reading *The Green Book*) is "thought that has not been thought out."

Like Homer's mythical Sirens, subjectivism calls to us with the appealing voice of enlightenment, science, culture, maturity, unsentimental rationality. We are told that only unsophisticated and "unscientific"—or worse, arrogant and intolerant—people believe that we can know what is objectively right and wrong. Moral and religious values are simply a product (or, worse, an accidental by-product) of evolution that must somehow have helped our ancestors and their civilizations to survive and thrive.[3] The problem with such a view, however, is that it is either inconsistent—one cannot deny knowledge of objective morality and at the same time claim that there is anything objectively wrong with being arrogant or intolerant—or it is viciously absurd, since it entails that we cannot know there to be anything objectively wrong with even the most horrendous evils.

For many contemporaries of Lewis, subjectivism had an allure of "scientific" sophistication, partly due to the rise in popularity of a related philosophical view known as logical positivism. One of the foremost proponents of logical positivism was the British philosopher A.J. Ayer, who published his famous book *Language, Truth, and Logic* in 1936 while a lecturer at Christ Church College, Oxford (just a short walk from Lewis' Magdalen College).[4] According to Ayer's famous "Principle of Verification," the only statements that have any literal meaning at all are tautologies such as "All bachelors are unmarried" and empirically verifiable statements. All other kinds of statements, Ayer argued, do not even rise to the level of being false—they are literally meaningless. In particular, Ayer held that all value claims and claims about God or about any other metaphysical entity are unscientific and meaningless. Ayer thus did not hold subjectivism about moral claims, since a moral statement that makes a claim about the speaker's emotions is still a meaningful claim. Instead, Ayer defended the subtly distinct view known as "emotivism." According to emotivism, when someone says that an action such as murder is wrong, she is not making a claim about her emotions toward that action as subjectivism suggests ("I have a feeling of disapproval about murder"), but rather simply expressing a negative emotion toward the action ("Murder . . . boo!"). As Ayer explains,

> . . . if I say to someone, "You acted wrongly in stealing that money," I am not stating anything more than if I had simply said, "You stole that money." In adding that this action is wrong I am not making any further statement about it. I am simply evincing my moral disapproval of it. It is as if I had said, "You stole that money," in a particular tone of horror, or written it with the addition of some special exclamation marks. The tone, or the exclamation marks, adds nothing to the literal meaning of the sentence. It merely serves to show that the expression of it is attended by certain feelings in the speaker.
>
> 1952, p. 107

One obvious problem with emotivism about moral statements and its close cousin subjectivism is that they are presumptuous. Who is the philosopher to determine what ordinary people mean when they make moral claims? Many, if not most, people who say that racial segregation is unjust, or that it is wrong to steal, mean to be making a claim about the wrongness of racial segregation and stealing, not just to be expressing their emotions (or, *pace* subjectivism, making a claim about their emotions). At least, that is certainly what I mean to be doing when I make such claims and I take it that I am at least as good of a judge of what I mean as anyone else.

Another and deeper problem is that the verificationist principle at the heart of logical positivism, versions of which seem to be taken by emotivists and subjectivists alike to lend scientific sophistication to their views, is self-refuting. The principle of verification is neither a tautology nor an empirically verifiable claim. The principle of verification is thus like the statement "All English sentences are meaningless"—if it is true, it is literally meaningless, neither true nor false. According to the law of non-contradiction, however, a proposition cannot be both true and not true at the same time. It seems that logical rigor has been sacrificed on the altar of pseudo-scientific sophistication.

Of course, Lewis recognized that in addition to being philosophically bankrupt, subjectivism has dangerous practical consequences. The Sirens of subjectivism call us to our death. We cannot give up on the possibility of objective moral knowledge, as so many sophomoric college students confidently and proudly claim to have done, without undercutting our ability to know that the Holocaust, the Rwandan genocide, American slavery, and the terrorist attacks on New York on 9/11, and on Beirut, Paris, Nigeria, and Mali in November 2015, were horrendously evil, inhumane, and unjust. No appeal to our subjective, "unimportant" feelings and, as Lewis points out, not even an appeal to our evolved "instincts" of self-preservation or the preservation of the species can give us grounds for claiming that such things *ought* not to be done. "From propositions about fact alone no *practical* conclusion can ever be drawn. *This will preserve society* cannot lead to *do this* except by the mediation of *society ought to be preserved*" (Lewis, 2001a, pp. 31–32, italics in original).

If we judge that such things as the Holocaust, the Rwandan genocide, American slavery, and radical Islamic terrorism ought not to be done, it is only because we are listening to the echo of the voice of Reason proclaiming the objective truth of the natural moral law—"the *Tao*"—that all people are created equal and endowed with the basic human rights to life and liberty (cf. Lewis, 2001a, p. 62). In fact, one of the unintended benefits to the human race of the horrendous evils of genocide, terrorism, rape, and murder is that they pierce our hard hearts, awakening our moral sensibilities, helping us to hear the voice of Reason through the intoxicating song of the subjectivist Sirens. As Lewis writes in *The Problem of Pain*, "God whispers to us in our pleasures, speaks in our conscience, but shouts in our pain: it is His megaphone to rouse a deaf world" (2001b, p. 91). It is easy enough to presume to be enlightened and rational when one is espousing moral subjectivism and skepticism in the context of the abstract debates that often take place in introduction to ethics courses, coffee shops, and on social media forums. It is much harder to sound enlightened and rational (or even human) when one espouses moral subjectivism and skepticism while standing amongst the dilapidated barracks of Auschwitz or at Ground Zero in New York. It may be, in fact, that the tragic recurrence of such violent, brutal, and destructive acts are all that have kept the global community tethered to the mast of moral knowledge in the decades since Lewis penned the prophetic words of *The Abolition of Man*. As a professor of ethics, however, semester after semester I encounter bright, well-meaning college students, who find it increasingly difficult to claim that there is (or that they know that there is) anything objectively wrong with even the most horrific acts of genocide and terrorism. In the end, the Sirens' subjectivist song, if not silenced, threatens to render our society deaf to the life-giving song of objective morality.

On seeing goodness, truth, and beauty with the eyes of the heart

But how can we silence the Sirens' song? How can we learn to hear more clearly the voice of Reason that sings the knowledge of objective morality? Fortunately, Lewis points us toward an answer to these questions. *The Abolition of Man* is not only a prophetic warning against sailing toward the song of subjectivism; it is also a compass that we can use to chart a course back to the knowledge of objective morality, if only we knew how to read it. Unfortunately, the key to reading *The Abolition of Man* is often missed. That is because the key to reading *The Abolition of Man* has to do with the emotions, which are widely misunderstood in modern (or, if you prefer, postmodern) Western society.

In development of their subjectivism, Gaius and Titius claim that emotions are not only unimportant, but also inherently irrational—mere sentimentality. In reply, Lewis grants that Gaius and Titius are likely motivated by the good intention of protecting students against being manipulated by emotional propaganda, but he disagrees that the way to protect them is by training them to distrust, if not to quell entirely, all emotions. Lewis writes,

> My own experience as a teacher tells an opposite tale. For every one pupil who needs to be guarded from a weak excess of sensibility there are three who need to be awakened from the slumber of cold vulgarity. The task of the modern educator is not to cut down jungles but to irrigate deserts. The right defence against false sentiments is to inculcate just sentiments. By starving the sensibility of our pupils we only make them easier prey to the propagandist when he comes. For famished nature will be avenged and a hard heart is no infallible protection against a soft head.
>
> 2001a, pp. 13–14

The upshot of Lewis' criticism against Gaius and Titius is this: teaching students an incorrect view of the nature of emotions can lead to improper formation of potentially valuable emotion-dispositions. In short, emotional miseducation breeds emotional malformation. As Lewis puts it, "Gaius and Titius, while teaching him nothing about letters, have cut out of [the pupil's] soul, long before he is old enough to choose, the possibility of having certain experiences which thinkers of more authority than they have held to be generous, fruitful, and humane" (2001a, p. 9).

Lewis' critique of *The Green Book* suggests that proper emotional formation relies on an implicit commitment to, if not explicit education about, an accurate understanding of emotions. Just what is the correct view of emotions then, that Lewis takes to be inextricably tied to proper emotional formation? Lewis describes it thus:

> Until quite modern times all teachers and even all men believed the universe to be such that certain emotional reactions on our part could be either congruous or incongruous to it—believed, in fact, that objects did not merely receive, but could merit, our approval or disapproval, our reverence or our contempt.
>
> 2001a, pp. 14–15

Lewis thus endorses a view of emotions according to which emotions are more or less accurate, apt or inapt responses to objective values in the world. He explains,

> . . . because our approvals and disapprovals are thus recognitions of objective value or responses to an objective order, therefore emotional states can be in harmony with reason (when we feel liking for what ought to be approved) or out of harmony with reason (when we perceive that liking is due but cannot feel it). No emotion is, in itself, a judgement; in that sense all emotions and sentiments are alogical. But they can be reasonable or unreasonable as they conform to Reason or fail to conform.
>
> 2001a, p. 19

Lewis' view of emotions as "recognitions of objective value" bears a close affinity to perceptual accounts of emotion that have been defended in recent literature by a growing number of philosophers and psychologists (see, for example, Frijda and Mesquita, 2000; Roberts, 2003; Zagzebski, 2004, ch. 2). According to such accounts, emotions are perception-like experiences of objective values. On perceptual accounts, emotions, like sense perceptions, can get things right or wrong and the wise and virtuous person will not only make the appropriate moral and aesthetic judgments, she will also "see" the value in the world accurately through her emotions. In keeping with a perceptual account of emotions, Lewis not only rejects Gaius and Titius's claim that all statements of value are merely reports of the speaker's emotions and that value statements are, therefore, unimportant; he also rejects their claim that emotions are inherently irrational. Indeed, from "Men Without Chests" we learn that emotions can be rational responses to objective values in the world.

While most sympathetic readers of *The Abolition of Man* appreciate the point of Lewis' arguments against subjectivism, few appreciate his account of the epistemology of emotions. Yet, Lewis' discussion of emotion in "Men Without Chests" suggests that if we want to preserve moral knowledge in society, it is not enough to debunk the subjectivist's mistaken view of moral judgments and emotions; moral educators—whether they be parents, teachers, pastors, counselors, or professors—also need to revive the ancient wisdom that emotions, as perception-like experiences of value, must work together with reason to give rise to knowledge of objective moral value and the natural moral law (i.e., "the *Tao*"). As Lewis puts it, paraphrasing Aristotle, "When the age for reflective thought comes, the pupil who has been thus trained in 'ordinate affections' or 'just sentiments' will easily find the first principles of Ethics; but to the corrupt man they will never be visible at all and he can make no progress in that science" (2001a, p. 16).

On the view Lewis here endorses, emotions, while not themselves judgments or beliefs, often help to form (and inform) our beliefs about moral and other values by helping us to "see" those values. In other words, our emotions present their objects to us as being valuable or disvaluable in some particular way, and we often trust our emotions by believing that things really are as our emotions present them to be. According to Lewis, trusting our emotions in this way is not always irrational or otherwise cognitively defective. In fact, when our emotions are properly formed, they enable direct awareness and, hence, knowledge of objective value.[5]

Lewis is not denying, nor would I, that emotions can and often do mislead us, such as when we get angry at minor offenses, when we fear things that are not dangerous, and when we admire those who are not worthy of admiration. He is certainly aware of the dangers of trusting misleading emotions, as evidenced by his concerns about emotionally manipulative propaganda, but rather than attempting to avoid such dangers by distrusting all emotions and thereby failing to attend to the difficult project of emotional formation, Lewis challenges educators to learn how to cultivate character traits that dispose us to have virtuous emotions—"just sentiments"—that reliably represent the objective values in the world. By "irrigating" students' arid hearts in this way, we can help them to experience or "see" the injustice of apartheid, the inhumanity of genocide, the beauty of a Beethoven symphony, the elegance of the physical laws of the universe, the dignity of all human persons, and even the grace and goodness of God through well-formed emotional perceptions—through, in particular, indignation, moral horror, aesthetic awe, wonder, love, contrition, and gratitude, respectively.

Lewis' claim that properly formed emotions can function together with reason as a perceptual source of moral knowledge is often missed by casual readers of *The Abolition of Man* and Lewis scholars alike. In his chapter in a volume on the philosophy of C.S. Lewis, for example, Peter Kreeft claims that "Lewis shocks us psychologistic moderns, us feeling-fondlers, by telling us, as do all the saints, that feelings, the powers by which we become aware of and attracted to beauty, are irrelevant and unimportant for moral goodness" (2008, p. 34). If Kreeft meant to argue that mere physiological "feelings" like a churning of the gut, racing of the heart, or tingling sensation are irrelevant to morality, then surely he is right, but that he has in mind more cognitive, perceptual "feelings" or emotions is suggested by his concession that such feelings can help us to become aware of aesthetic values. Thus, it seems that Kreeft takes Lewis' remarks in "Men Without Chests" concerning the nature of emotions as perceptions ("recognitions") of value to be relevant to aesthetic value alone, as opposed to the objective moral law and moral value on which Lewis focuses throughout the remainder of the book.

Although Lewis' primary examples of emotional perceptions of value in "Men Without Chests" have to do with aesthetic value, the view of emotions he endorses in the essay naturally suggests, *pace* Kreeft, that when emotions are functioning properly they can be important sources of awareness and, therefore, knowledge of moral as well as aesthetic value. Indeed, the insight that emotions can make us aware of moral as well as aesthetic values seems to underlie the severity of Lewis' warning that we do children a great disservice if we teach them to distrust their emotions, thereby creating generations of people devoid of well-formed emotional sensitivities—people, as Lewis puts it, "without chests." Lewis' worry is not merely that students with poorly formed emotions will miss out on experiences (and knowledge) of aesthetic beauty, but also that they will fail to recognize and appreciate moral goodness and the value of truth as well. Having been hypnotized by the song of the Sirens, those who embrace subjectivism will fail to develop the ears to hear the voice of Reason; they will fail to develop the ability to "see" goodness, truth, and beauty with the eye of their hearts.

Concerning the importance of apt emotions ("just sentiments") for maintaining an appreciative awareness of the value of truth—the heart of all intellectual virtue—Lewis writes, "a persevering devotion to truth, a nice sense of intellectual honour, cannot be long maintained without the aid of a sentiment which Gaius and Titius could debunk as well as any other" (2001, p. 25). For Lewis, then, it seems that emotions help us to recognize or perceive all kinds of value, including aesthetic and moral as well as epistemic or alethic value.[6] Indeed, it would be a bit surprising if Lewis had argued that emotions are recognitions of aesthetic value, but that they are irrelevant to perceiving moral and other kinds of value, given his emphasis throughout his fictional and non-fictional writings on the interconnectedness of the Good, the True, and the Beautiful.

Lewis' overarching argument in *The Abolition of Man*, which he develops over the three essays, thus seems to proceed as follows: (1) Since emotions are our primary mode of directly experiencing or perceiving objective moral as well as other kinds of value, undermining young people's trust in their emotional perceptions of value (rendering them "Men Without Chests") inevitably leads to (2) widespread skepticism concerning the objective moral law ("The Way"), which, in turn, leads to (3) an unbridled quest to conquer and manipulate all of nature, including our own human nature, to serve our basest appetites ("The Abolition of Man"). Reading "Men Without Chests" as an essay concerning the importance of emotions as a source of cognitive access to objective morality as well as other kinds of value thus provides literary cohesion to the book as a whole.

The importance of emotions for Lewis' argument in *The Abolition of Man* is perhaps muddied by the fact that he claims to be in agreement about the relationship between emotions and reason and about the natural moral law with a number of philosophers whose views on these matters differ considerably—most notably, Plato, Aristotle, Augustine, John Locke, and Confucius.[7] Whereas Aristotle seems to have thought that virtuous emotions contribute to the perceptual function of practical wisdom, Plato and Augustine seem to be less inclined to grant emotions a positive epistemic role in the achievement of moral knowledge. Plato, in particular, believed that humans could know objective morality—what is right, wrong, just, unjust—and that moral character formation involves learning to love what is good and detest what is evil, but he held that the street connecting Reason and emotion is ideally only one-way. Plato held a "tripartite theory of the soul," according to which the soul is composed of Reason, Spirit (the seat of the emotions), and Appetite, which he depicts in his *Republic* as a human being, a lion, and a multi-headed monster, respectively (Plato, 1992, book IX, 588–589; Lewis, 2001b, pp. 260–261). According to Plato, the just or virtuous person's soul is characterized by Reason ruling and using the emotional sentiments of the Spirit to help tame and cultivate the Appetites. As Lewis summarizes Plato's view, "the head rules the belly through the chest" (2001a, p. 24). Locke likewise believed that humans have a faculty of reason by which they can know the natural moral law, but the emotions do not seem to have played an important role in his epistemology. As Locke explains, "The state of nature has a law of nature to govern it, which obliges everyone: and reason, which is that law, teaches all mankind, who will but consult it, that being all equal and independent, no one ought to harm another in his life, health, liberty, or possessions" (1980, p. 9).

What Lewis takes all of these philosophers to have in common is that they believed in objective value, that we could know objective value (including the natural moral law), and that the presence of objective value in the world makes certain emotions, desires, or loves appropriate and others inappropriate. Lewis explains,

> Those who know the *Tao* can hold that to call children delightful or old men venerable is not simply to record a psychological fact about our own parental or filial emotions at the moment, but to recognize a quality which demands a certain response from us whether we make it or not.
>
> 2001a, p. 19

If my argument in this section is correct, Lewis differs from at least some of these philosophers (perhaps agreeing most closely with Aristotle) in thinking that emotions have an important epistemic role to play in helping us to recognize, and hence to know, objective moral value and the natural moral law. Lewis' own view seems to have been that there are some foundational truths of morality (e.g., the Golden Rule, or that murder is unjust, or that it is noble to sacrifice one's life for one's friend) that are quite obviously true and that need no argument or proof, but that the faculty through which we grasp such truths, which Lewis often refers to simply as "Reason," is essentially emotional reason, rational sentiment, or "feeling intellect."[8] The reason it seems obvious to us that murder, rape, and terrorism are (objectively) unjust and evil is that we experience strong emotions of indignation and moral horror toward murder, rape, and acts of terror. Put slightly differently, the experience of such rational emotions is just what it is for such moral principles to seem obviously true to us. Gilbert Meilaender puts the point just right in his articulation of Lewis' view:

> Moral insight, therefore, is not a matter for reason alone; it requires trained emotions and moral habits of behavior inculcated even before we reach an age of reason. "The head rules the belly through the chest." Reason disciplines appetite only with the aid of trained emotions. It turns out, then, that moral education does more than simply enable us to "see" what virtue requires. It also enables us, at least to some extent, to *be* virtuous. For the very training

> of the emotions that makes insight possible will have produced in us traits of character that incline us to love the good and do it.
>
> 2010, pp. 124–125

Emotional formation is thus constitutive of moral education not only in the sense that developing well-formed emotion-dispositions is part of what it is to become more morally virtuous, but also in the sense that accurate emotional perceptions can inform moral knowledge and moral understanding (i.e., wisdom). By educating for emotional formation, therefore, we educate both the head and the heart.

Emotional cultivation versus conditioning

In his critique of subjectivism in "Men Without Chests," Lewis briefly explains that his account of emotions and moral knowledge (informed as it is by the wisdom of the ancients) encourages a dramatically different approach to moral education and moral formation than the approach that follows from subjectivism. He explains,

> When a Roman father told his son that it was a sweet and seemly thing to die for his country, he believed what he said. He was communicating to the son an emotion which he himself shared and which he believed to be in accord with the value which his judgement discerned in noble death. But Gaius and Titius cannot believe that in calling such a death sweet and seemly they would be saying "something important about something."
>
> 2001a, pp. 22–23

Indeed, whereas Plato, Aristotle, Augustine, Locke, and Confucius believed that some emotions are appropriate or fitting responses to the objective value in the world while others are not, the value-debunking subjectivist holds that emotions are unimportant if not irrational. The obvious problem for moral education is that if subjectivism is true, then either all moral and aesthetic emotions ("sentiments") will be debunked and discouraged as equally irrational and unimportant, or some emotions will be debunked while others are encouraged, though there is nothing more "just" or "ordinate" or objectively right about the latter class of emotions than there is about the former.

Of course, Gaius and Titius, like most educators in their better moments, think that some emotions ought to be encouraged and others discouraged. Likewise, even many of the staunchest value-debunkers of today think that there really is something detestable about racist discrimination, sexual assault, and bullying. The eighteenth-century Scottish "common sense" philosopher, Thomas Reid, once described those skeptical philosophers who claim not to believe their sense perception of the external world, while maintaining belief in the deliverances of reason and introspection, as inconsistent "semi-skeptics" (1997, p. 71). Gaius and Titius and their ilk are likewise inconsistent semi-subjectivists. The educational problem for such inconsistent semi-subjectivists is that they, unlike the philosophers Lewis cites, cannot appeal to the justness or rightness of having one emotion or another; rather, if they are to encourage an emotion they can only do so through a non-rational or, worse, irrational process of "conditioning." Lewis explains,

> If they embark on this course the difference between the old and the new education will be an important one. Where the old initiated, the new merely "conditions." The old dealt with its pupils as grown birds deal with young birds when they teach them to fly; the new deals with them more as the poultry-keeper deals with young birds—making them thus or thus for purposes of which the birds know nothing. In a word, the old *was* a kind of propagation—men transmitting manhood to men; the new is merely propaganda.
>
> 2001a, pp. 22–23

Lewis was no doubt familiar with Ivan Pavlov's famous experiments involving the conditioning of dogs. In classical behaviorist conditioning, a subject (in Pavlov's case, the dog) is presented with an unconditioned stimulus (food) that triggers an unconditioned response (salivation). Then, the experimenter introduces a neutral stimulus (like the sound of a bell) that, with repeated experience, the subject begins to associate or "pair" with the unconditioned stimulus. Once such association or pairing has become entrenched in the subject's psychology, the once neutral stimulus (the sound of the bell) now triggers the conditioned response (salivation) even without the presence of the unconditioned stimulus (food).

Psychologists building on Pavlov's work discovered that a similar "conditioning" process could be used to pair emotional responses with previously neutral stimuli. In one famous experiment, a nine-month-old baby, Albert, was introduced to a white rat (neutral stimulus), which he was not initially afraid of (Watson and Rayner, 1920). But then the experimenters repeatedly paired the presentation of the white rat to Albert with a loud noise (unconditioned stimulus) that scared Albert (unconditioned response). Eventually, Albert would respond in fear when presented with the white rat, as well as other white objects, even in the absence of the scary noise. Albert's "fear of the white rat" (or fear of whiteness) was thus a conditioned emotional response.[9]

Lewis keenly recognized that if subjectivism is true, emotional education will be reduced to just such a process of conditioning. Of course, the problem with conditioning is that conditioned responses are lacking in moral content and moral understanding (i.e., wisdom). If Albert really is afraid of the white rat, then his fear is irrational—there is nothing particularly dangerous or threatening about the rat. Fear is not a "just" or fitting response to the rat. Of course, Albert might not be afraid of the rat at all. It might be that Albert has come to experience the rat as a reliable sign of something else that is dangerous and threatening—the loud, scary noise. If that is the case, then Albert's fear reflects a modicum of understanding, but it is understanding of a contrived experimental environment that does not reflect the way things are in the real world—white rats aren't naturally dangerous or harbingers of danger. Insofar as the conditioning process has "paired" Albert's fear with the stimulus of the rat, it has taught him absolutely nothing about what is objectively worth fearing. Likewise, if an educator succeeds in conditioning certain moral emotional responses (awe, disgust, guilt, admiration) by evoking those emotional responses through the use of unconditioned stimuli and then "pairing" them with the objects toward which the conditioner wants the subject to feel them, a kind of emotional formation has happened, but the student is none the wiser and his soul is no more human as a result. He is like a dog that finds itself salivating when a bell is rung.

Contrast such emotional conditioning with the ancient practice of emotional cultivation (what Lewis calls "propagation"). Since emotions are perceptions of value that aid in and manifest our understanding of that value, moral educators ought to encourage the development of "just" emotions by helping students to "see" and understand the value (or disvalue) of the emotions' proper objects.

Rather than conditioning students so that when they encounter racial injustice of one kind or another it triggers feelings of indignation (absent any understanding on the student's part), true moral education must involve explaining to students just what is so unjust or immoral about racism so that they learn to see it for themselves. When they have come to appreciate the equal dignity and worth of all people and when they have learned to recognize the various insidious features of racial injustice, they will feel indignation and anger toward such injustice because they see it (and understand it) as the evil it truly is. When they have come to appreciate the beauty and majesty of the natural world, they will see it as it truly is through the eyes of awe and wonder. When they have learned to love moral goodness, they will see the generous, the compassionate, the kind, the humble, the gentle, and the just as they truly are through the eyes of admiration and gratitude.

The student with well-formed emotions will have eyes to see and ears to hear the voice of Reason singing the song of objective moral value, and she will not be tempted by the Sirens of subjectivism to sail toward the island of the abolition of man. She will see the value of true emotional cultivation and thus will decry the moral bankruptcy of emotional conditioning; she will see the dignity of all people, even those precious little ones whose dignity is veiled by a mother's womb, and thus will fight to protect them from eugenic programs of genetic selection and manipulation; she will see the beauty and elegance of the natural world and thus will resist its total conquest and destruction in service of human "progress" and economic efficiency; she will love what is good and hate what is evil, and and she will know the difference because she will feel it.[10]

Notes

1 These are Lewis' own examples from *Miracles* (1996, p. 51).

2 For Lewis' discussion of Gaius and Titius's value system, see Lewis (2001a, p. 105, note 1).

3 See, for example, Jonathan Haidt's (2012) influential evolutionary psychology of moral and religious values. For a critical discussion of Haidt's account of the origin of moral and religious values, see Pelser and Roberts (2015).

4 Interestingly, the British philosopher Antony Flew originally presented his now-famous critique of Ayer's logical positivism, "Theology and Falsification," at a meeting of the Oxford Socratic Club chaired by C.S. Lewis, though Lewis had

already published *The Abolition of Man*. Flew recounts his interactions with Lewis and the development of his famous paper in an interview with Gary Habermas in Flew and Habermas (2008, pp. 37–39).

5 It is important to note here that I am not claiming, nor would Lewis claim, that emotions actually create or serve as the metaphysical ground of value in the world. On my view, which I take to be shared by Lewis, emotions help us to experience and thus to know or understand *objective* values—that is, values that exist in the world independently of our emotions and other mental states.

6 Here "epistemic value" (from the Greek *episteme*, meaning knowledge or understanding) refers to the value of our cognitive grasp of truth or reality, while "alethic value" (from the Greek *alethia*, meaning truth) refers to the special value of truth itself.

7 For those who are surprised that Lewis, a Christian, would claim to be in agreement with the moral philosophy of Confucius, see Ten Elshof (2015).

8 I have this phrase from Carnell (1974).

9 For an extended critique of the associationist psychology of emotions that underlies such emotional conditioning, see Pelser and Roberts (forthcoming).

10 The views expressed in this chapter are the author's own and do not necessarily reflect the official policies or positions of the US Air Force, the US Department of Defense, or the US government.

Works cited

Ayer, A.J. (1946 [1952]), *Language, Truth and Logic* (2nd edn.). New York: Dover.

Carnell, C.S. (1974), *Bright Shadow of Reality: C.S. Lewis and the Feeling Intellect.* Grand Rapids, MI: Eerdmans.

Chesterton, G.K. (1950), "The revival of philosophy—why?," in *The Common Man.* London: Sheed & Ward, pp. 173–180.

Elshtain, J.B. (2008), "*The Abolition of Man*: C.S. Lewis' prescience concerning things to come," in D. Baggett, G.R. Habermas and J.L. Walls (eds.), *C.S. Lewis as Philosopher: Truth, Goodness and Beauty.* Downers Grove, IL: IVP Academic, pp. 85–95.

Flew, A. and Habermas, G.R. (2008), "From atheism to deism: A conversation between Antony Flew and Gary R. Habermas," in D. Baggett, G.R. Habermas and J.L. Walls (eds.), *C.S. Lewis as Philosopher: Truth, Goodness and Beauty.* Downers Grove, IL: IVP Academic, pp. 37–52.

Frijda, N. and Mesquita, B. (2000), "Beliefs through emotions," in N. Frijda, A.S.R. Manstead and S. Bemet (eds.), *Emotions and Beliefs: How Feelings Influence Thoughts.* Cambridge: Cambridge University Press, pp. 45–77.

Haidt, J. (2012), *The Righteous Mind: Why Good People are Divided by Politics and Religion*. New York: Pantheon Books.

Kreeft, P. (1994), *C.S. Lewis for the Third Millenium*. San Francisco, CA: Ignatius Press.

Kreeft, P. (2008), "Lewis' philosophy of truth, goodness and beauty," in D. Baggett, G.R. Habermas and J.L. Walls (eds.), *C.S. Lewis as Philosopher: Truth, Goodness and Beauty*. Downers Grove, IL: IVP Academic, pp. 23–36.

Lewis, C.S. (1996), *Miracles*. New York: Touchstone.

Lewis, C.S. (2001a), *The Abolition of Man—Or Reflections on Education with Special Reference to the Teaching of English in the Upper Forms of Schools*. San Francisco, CA: HarperCollins.

Lewis, C.S. (2001b), *The Problem of Pain*. San Francisco, CA: HarperCollins.

Locke, J. (1690 [1980]), *Second Treatise of Government* (ed. C.B. Macpherson). Indianapolis, IN: Hackett.

Meilaender, G. (2010), "On moral knowledge," in R. MacSwain and M. Ward (eds.), *The Cambridge Companion to C.S. Lewis*. Cambridge: Cambridge University Press, pp. 119–131.

Pelser, A.C. (2014), "Irrigating Deserts: Thinking with C.S. Lewis about Educating for Emotional Formation," *Christian Scholar's Review*, 44, 27–43.

Pelser, A.C. and Roberts, R.C. (2015), "Religious value and moral psychology," in T. Brosch and D. Sander (eds.), *Handbook of Value: Perspectives from Economics, Neuroscience, Philosophy, Psychology, and Sociology*. Oxford: Oxford University Press, pp. 375–394.

Pelser, A.C. and Roberts, R.C. (forthcoming), "Emotions, character, and associationist psychology," *Journal of Moral Philosophy*.

Plato (1992), *Republic* (trans. G.M.A. Grube, revised by C.D.C. Reeve). Indianapolis, IN: Hackett.

Reid, T. (1997), *An Inquiry into the Human Mind on the Principles of Common Sense*. University Park, PA: Pennsylvania State University Press.

Roberts, R.C. (2003), *Emotions: An Essay in Aid of Moral Psychology*. Cambridge: Cambridge University Press.

Smith, C., Christofferseon, K., Davidson, H. and Snell Herzog, P. (2011), *Lost in Transition: The Dark Side of Emerging Adulthood*. Oxford: Oxford University Press.

Ten Elshof, G.A. (2015), *Confucius for Christians: What an Ancient Chinese Worldview can Teach Us about Life in Christ*. Grand Rapids, MI: Eerdmans.

Watson, J.B. and Rayner, R. (1920), "Conditioned emotional reactions," *Journal of Experimental Psychology*, 3, 1–13.

Zagzebski, L.T. (2004), *Divine Motivation Theory*. Cambridge: Cambridge University Press.

2

Natural Law in *The Abolition of Man*

Micah Watson
Calvin College

Of Dwarfs, prisons, and the natural law

We find an important clue to understanding Lewis' defense of natural law in *The Abolition of Man* in what may seem an unlikely source in Lewis' corpus. Near the conclusion of *The Last Battle*, Lewis' apocalyptic conclusion to the Chronicles of Narnia, the fighting is over and Aslan has joined the last kings and queens of Narnia. The forces of evil have been defeated, goodness has prevailed, and all that remains is to pass into Aslan's country for eternity. Yet one troubling plot point remains unresolved.

The treacherous Dwarfs are determined to snatch defeat from the jaws of victory. They refuse to be "taken in," and sit huddled and miserable in the dark confines of what they take to be a black hole. Queen Lucy, always Lewis' moral exemplar in the Narnia books, leads an effort to persuade the Dwarfs to see things as they really are. They are not in a black hole but in the midst of the open sky, the green grass, and fragrant flowers. Paradise awaits them if only they have eyes to see and ears to hear. Lucy tearfully begs Aslan to help the Dwarfs, and he provides them a sumptuous feast, but to no avail. Not even Aslan will force those who choose blindness to see what truly is. "They will not let us help them," Aslan says. "They have chosen cunning instead of belief. Their prison is only in their own minds, yet they are in that prison; and so afraid of being taken in that they cannot be taken out" (Lewis, 1984, pp. 180–186).

The Abolition of Man is about that prison. It is about the predicament of those people who do not merely misunderstand or misapply this or that moral teaching, but reject root and branch the very possibility of moral reality. To be sure Lewis' incisive three lectures are about many other things as well. There is a reason Walter Hooper claimed that *Abolition* is an all but indispensable introduction to the entire *corpus* of "Lewisiana" (Lewis, 1967, p. 47).

Yet we miss something crucial to understanding this work, and how to evaluate it, if we do not recognize from the outset Lewis' claims about the limits of reason and thus the limits of the efficacy of natural law. The same Lewis who is rightly regarded as a champion of reason and apologetics also repeatedly illustrates in his fiction and his straightforward works that there are some boundaries that reason cannot cross.

The Dwarfs are impervious to Lucy's attempts to reason with them, and Aslan himself will not force the issue. *The Great Divorce* features example after example of damned souls resisting grace-filled invitations to remain in Heaven, perhaps most powerfully illustrated in the conversation between the learned apostate Anglican bishop and his young interlocutor, Dick. Even in Heaven itself the eminently reasonable entreaties of Dick are lost on the bishop, and there is nothing for him except the bus ride back to Hell (Lewis, 1946, pp. 37–47). *Perelandra* features an ongoing chess-like debate between God's representative Ransom, and the Devil's agent Weston, sent to corrupt another unfallen planet. That dialectical discussion also fails to reconcile the two figures, and it is not the spoken word that delivers the decision to Ransom, but physical force. After reasoned argument has failed, Lewis' Ransom acts on God's behalf by killing the Devil-possessed Weston in the name of the Trinity and thereby preserving the innocence of Perelandra (Lewis, 1996a, pp. 181–182). Lewis depicts the limits of reason as much or more than its efficacy.

The potential of reason is undercut by the spirit of this age. As Screwtape explains in his opening letter to Wormwood, humans at one point "knew pretty well when a thing was proved and when it was not; and if it was proved they really believed it. They still connected thinking with doing and were prepared to alter their way of life as the result of a chain of reasoning" (Lewis, 1996b, pp. 1–2).[1] Actual argument threatens the cause of Hell, Screwtape continues, because it "moves the whole struggle onto the Enemy's own ground." Genuine argument is, after all, about determining the truth about a matter, and the Christian God is a God of truth. Better to prevent human beings from even flirting with arguments and reasons in the first place, lest they stumble upon the source of Truth that grounds all other truths. Keep them from foundational premises and the clever tempter can all but assure they will not arrive at any troubling conclusions.

Lewis' task in *Abolition* is delicate. If people have largely rejected the legitimacy of logical reasoning, how does one make the case for the proposition that the foundational building blocks of morality cannot be established by argument, but are nevertheless real? And not only real, but "the foundation of all clear thinking about ourselves and the universe we live in" (Lewis, 1960, p. 7). Moreover, how can we evaluate such a project? In the pages that follow, we will delve into the connections between Lewis' arguments in *Abolition*, the reality of natural law or the *Tao*, and natural law theory. We will find that while *Abolition* is a defense of natural law, it is not a work of natural law theory. First, we will briefly consider what natural law *is*, and what a natural law theory *does*. With some definitions in hand we will then be in a position to describe what Lewis is up to in the three lectures that comprise *Abolition* and how his project intersects with natural law theories. We will see that Lewis focuses on the foundations of natural law thinking because of modernity's unprecedented suspicion of reason, and that his defense of natural law is intended to expose rather than bridge the chasm between a humane moral realism and a post-human vision of brute power, directionless progress, and reductionist appropriation.

Natural law and natural law theory

What do we mean by natural law and natural law theory?[2] There is no way to give a definition without running afoul of one school of natural law or another. Nevertheless, natural law can be said to be natural in that it seeks to delineate the means by which persons can fulfill their telos given that they have an essential nature. It is law insofar as it is authored by a lawgiver and is meant to regulate behavior. Natural law *theory* is the attempt of philosophers to describe the various components of natural law: its source, its teleology, its precepts and how they are accessed (reasonable objectivity), its application, and its ramifications for political life.[3] Natural law theorists differ as to the details of these components, and natural law theories emphasize some of these aspects more than others. A quick word about each of these components will give us some context to help us describe how *Abolition* relates to natural law theory.

Source

The source of natural law is an ontological question. Most natural law theorists are also theists, describing the natural law as being authored by God and subsisting by his character and will. God acts as the architect who has placed the natural law in the ordering of the universe as well as in the hearts of humanity. Thomas Aquinas defines law as a "dictate of practical reason from the ruler who governs a perfect community" and eternal law is God's knowledge—as he knows it—regarding the governance of all reality. Natural law is a subset of eternal law; it is what human beings can know using their natural reasoning powers about God's law.[4] We might say here that Aquinas describes the source of natural law as residing in the mind of God and thus woven into the fabric of reality.

It is no surprise that Lewis agreed that God is the source of the natural law, not just because a law needs a lawgiver but because the goodness inherent in the natural law is somehow bound up with God's own character.[5] God is the author of the moral law, which reflects his character, as we see not only in Lewis' ethical writings like "On Ethics" and "The Poison of Subjectivism" but also in his apologetic strategy in the opening of *Mere Christianity*. It is worth noting, then, that Lewis' work in *Abolition* does not take up this question of what grounds the existence of the natural law or, to use Lewis' term, the *Tao*. In fact, he explicitly denies that he is attempting to lead his readers to theism via his argument.[6]

Teleology, moral precepts, and reasonable objectivity

To what sort of creatures does the natural law apply? What is the *nature* of beings for whom the natural law is directed and directive? When a natural lawyer considers a being's nature, a discussion of teleology or purpose is sure to follow. Aristotle is the great philosopher of purpose, giving such examples as health as the end of medicine, ships as the end of shipbuilding, victory as the end of strategy, and wealth as the end of economics (Aristotle, 1987, p. 1). To understand what a thing *is* requires understanding what its purpose is, what that thing is meant *to be*. Natural law theory presupposes that there is also an end or purpose for human beings, though not all natural law theorists agree on what that end is, or even whether it is a single end or a collection of ends. Though not strictly speaking a natural law theorist, Aristotle held that it was a certain kind of happiness or flourishing characterized by a life of virtue. Aquinas also believed humanity has a telos but that it was realized in relationship with God through the church. Proponents of the new natural law theory hold that there are numerous incommensurable human goods that can be incorporated in an infinite number of ways that are compatible with "integral human fulfillment," or a life well lived (Finnis *et al.*, 1987, p. 283). This aspect of natural law thinking addresses the question of what it looks like for a human being to have fulfilled her purpose.

One of the most contested claims of natural law theory is not only that humanity has a "built-in" telos and that there are objective standards of right and wrong, but that each person has access to this telos and the accompanying moral standards through their moral reason. This claim can be referred to as "reasonable objectivity." The natural law is *reasonable* because it pertains to people who can both apprehend the natural law through moral reason as well as repress it. They are rationale creatures whose fulfillment is found in achieving an end appropriate to their nature.

The natural law also includes moral content, goods that are to be practiced, evils that are to be avoided. By participating in genuine goods, human beings contribute to the fulfillment of their purpose just as participating in evil frustrates that same purpose.[7] The precepts of the natural law are *objective* because they exist apart from any person's subjective and experiential truth claims. Thus natural law theory runs counter to an emphasis on "personal truth" or perspectivalism. To sum up, natural law is addressed to rational human beings who have been created with a purpose and who can use their reason to not only discern that purpose but also understand what they should and should not do in pursuing the fulfillment of that purpose.

Application

Natural law theorists do not merely produce lists of required and prohibited actions. Human behavior is complex, and applying enduring moral standards to changing cultures and unforeseen circumstances requires careful thought and application. How do natural law principles apply to the new bioethics challenges of cloning and reproductive technology? Does the advent of the nuclear era introduce a new element to natural law thinking about just war? Can the use of nuclear weapons be just? Do changes in social attitudes toward homosexuality require new thinking about the normativity of sexual behavior? What does natural law teach with regard to human sexuality?

Natural law theory requires some means of working through these questions. It is not an archeological intellectual discipline in which scholars unearth the positions of what earlier thinkers have said, as if fidelity to the natural law was merely a matter of accepting wisdom from the past. The promise of natural law thinking is that we can use our reason to tap into and apply the truth about ourselves to questions of how we should live. What previous thinkers have said about this or that moral concern is an important factor in that process, but not definitive. And in some cases, such as nuclear deterrence and embryonic stem cell research, there simply is no direct precedent to consider. Part of a natural law theory, then, is articulating how one works from foundational principles of morality, given the realities of human nature, to concrete applications of that morality to real-life situations and problems. Hence we see contemporary natural law thinkers address age-old questions like the permissibility of lying as well as new questions of application like the justice of nuclear deterrence.[8] Natural law, in this respect, is one among many different schools in the discipline of applied ethics.

The common good

Natural law theory is a practical discipline. It has real life application and outcomes. What philosophers conclude about how the doctrine of double effect applies to military decisions does not stay confined to the ivory tower but will be taught in military academies and consulted by politicians and government officials. If natural lawyers are correct about the power of human reason to make sound moral judgments, this has significant consequences for how we think about common political commitments in an increasingly pluralistic public square. We need not agree on the particular metaphysics that underlie a commitment to human rights to agree on protecting human rights. And if it is true that human beings have a knowable telos and can know the sort of actions that contribute to a morally flourishing life, then natural law doctrine has enormous implications for education, for how human beings grow from helpless children to responsible and virtuous adults. All of these practical concerns speak to how natural law thinking plays out with regard to the political community. Here we see what is at stake for those societies and governments that accept—or reject—the truth about natural law and human nature.

Lewis' *Abolition* and natural law theory

We are now in a better position to characterize Lewis' project in *Abolition*. As already noted, *Abolition* does not address the relationship between the natural law and its creator or source as Lewis did in "The Poison of Subjectivism," nor does Lewis here invoke the natural law to introduce the idea of a moral law that we have all broken such that we need a savior, as he did in the opening chapters of *Mere Christianity*. We know from those works that Lewis was very interested in the divine-natural relationship, but for reasons we will get to, he pointedly avoided this facet of natural law thinking in *Abolition*.

Nor did Lewis offer a full-throated explication of a final cause for human beings, or what we might think of as the ultimate purpose. This point requires some care, as Lewis definitely assumes and defends the teleological notion that human beings are designed to become certain types of creatures. Education informed by the *Tao* hands on a way of life meant to shape people a particular way, a way not created but inherited. "It was but old birds teaching young birds to fly" (Lewis, 2001a, p. 61). *Abolition* is teleological, then, in that it assumes that people uninstructed in the natural law will fail to be who they are meant to be much as birds fall short of their nature as birds if they never learn to fly. But it is not teleological insofar as Lewis does not attempt to comprehensively describe what a flourishing human life looks like.[9] Nor does *Abolition* address fully the role of the natural law in fulfilling humanity's telos. In his other works, Lewis famously defends the Christian idea with which Augustine opens up his *Confessions* and the Westminster Shorter Catechism answers in its first question. We are created for eternal relationship with God, our hearts being restless until they rest with him, and the chief end of man being to worship God and enjoy him forever.[10] Yet as important as this theme was for Lewis the Christian apologist, *Abolition* does not address it at all.

The same holds true for application. While Lewis does mention several clear and concrete duties in *Abolition*, such as many listed in the appendix and the often referred to good of dying for one's country, there is no description of how we are to work through the thorny problems of applying natural law to actual political and moral dilemmas and situations. The closest we get in Lewis' corpus to a sort of program of ethical casuistry is found in Lewis' 1940 address to the Oxford Pacifist Society, "Why I am not a Pacifist" (Lewis, 2001b, pp. 64–90). There he goes into some detail as to how we make moral judgments at all, and addresses the role of basic moral premises and how one applies facts and appeals to authority in coming to one's moral conclusion. Lewis certainly understood the importance of working through the casuistry of moral judgment, but he did not see it as his particular assignment, and certainly not in *Abolition*. He was up to something different.

We see the difference when we consider the remaining three components of natural law theory: moral precepts, reasonable objectivity, and the common good. Here we see a great deal of resonance between these subjects and the three chapters of *Abolition*. Lewis does look at moral precepts. He claims these precepts are objectively true regardless of how we *feel* about them, and that it is part of the essence of human nature itself to be able to apprehend moral truths. Moreover, Lewis' opening chapter "Men Without Chests" speaks to the common good by provocatively describing the consequences for a society that abandons the moral law. Thus we do see some elements of natural law theorizing present in *Abolition*.

Nevertheless, by looking at these chapters we can also understand that *Abolition* is not a formal work of natural law theory, and thus cannot be evaluated as such. Lewis is more of a natural law apologist than he is a natural law theorist. He is a *mere* natural lawyer if you like. He is not building a theory so much as revealing a choice between incommensurable and radical (to the root) commitments. His case for the natural law is somewhat paradoxical, as it must be if he is correct about the nature of the first principles or primeval moral values that must be accepted before any genuinely moral reasoning can take place.

From Lewis' perspective, writing a book of natural law theory when many people question the very foundations of morality itself would be (at least for him) something of a fool's errand. One doesn't write chess manuals for those who see games as a complete waste of time. One cannot prescribe medical remedies to those who reject health as a good. One doesn't write about literary criticism for an audience that cannot see the point of reading a book. One has to first write about the intrinsic good of play, the good of health, and the good of art. Only if those basic premises are accepted can one have a conversation, or even an argument, about games, medicine, and books.

But now we are back to the dilemma with which this chapter opened. How does one argue for first principles? In an essay entitled "Miracles" that strongly parallels themes in *Abolition*, Lewis describes the difficulty he's trying to solve, and notes that appealing to experience is not a fool-proof method:

> Experience by itself proves nothing. If a man doubts whether he is dreaming or waking, no experiment can solve his doubt, since every experiment may itself be part of the dream. Experience proves this, or that, or nothing, according to the preconceptions we bring to it.
>
> 1989, pp. 25–26

The preconceptions we bring to moral reasoning, however, are themselves what philosophers call basic, *per se nota*, or self-evident. This has nothing to do with their being obvious or simple, but rather that there is no more fundamental ground that their validity relies on. Lewis confirms this not only in "The Way" and the appendix in *Abolition*, but in his book (not the essay) *Miracles*:

> . . . the primary moral principles on which all others depend are rationally perceived. We "just see" that there is no reason why my neighbour's happiness should be sacrified to my own, as we "Just see" that things which are equal to the same thing are equal to one another. If we cannot prove either axiom, it is not because they are irrational. It is because they are self-evident, and all proofs depend on them. Their intrinsic reasonableness shines by its own light.
>
> 1978, pp. 34–35

To not see that reasonableness is to be, like the Narnian Dwarfs, blind. This observation about self-evident truths is hardly unique to Lewis, nor is the challenge of how to illustrate the truth of first principles without appealing to some more fundamental truth. John Finnis faced the same challenge in presenting the good of knowledge as basic in his *Natural Law and Natural Rights* (1980). Finnis's approach did appeal to his reader's experience, albeit not to prove the good of knowledge but to reveal that the reader already accepted that knowledge was a basic good. He did this by interrogating the very practice that the reader was engaging in by reading and trying to understand Finnis's book.[11]

Like Finnis, Lewis also takes a novel tack in making the case for the *Tao*. He is not attempting to prove the validity of natural law—a quixotic task—but rather using the power of reason to illustrate the alternatives to a belief in foundational moral principles. Much like Finnis's strategy in his work, Lewis hopes to awaken a realization in his readers that they do, after all, believe in the natural law. He does this differently in each chapter, laying out in "Men Without Chests" a Platonic and Aristotelian picture of the human person as well as the high stakes for moral education in the political community. In "The Way," Lewis dissects any attempt to extract one isolated component of natural law and build a "new" ethic by exalting it over the others. And the chapter "The Abolition of Man" does not so much present the positive case for natural law as it does reveal the stark and—to a minimally decent moral person—horrific alternative.

"Men without Chests"

One thing should quickly become clear about the rather odd way in which Lewis begins his defense of the *Tao* in "Men without Chests": this is a fighting book, and Lewis thinks the stakes are enormous. In emphasizing the importance of children's schoolbooks, Lewis adopts a polite tone in his treatment of what he calls *The Green Book* and courteously avoids mentioning the authors by name. Just beneath the surface of this politeness, however, there are not-so-subtle signs of just how much Lewis disdained the project of Gaius and Titius and feared its consequences. The epigram on the title page likens the authors to Herod, who ordered the slaughter of baby boys and toddlers in an attempt to murder the Christ child.[12] Lewis goes on to note the dishonesty of passing off an emotivist philosophy of language under the cover of English grammar and writing (Lewis, 2001a, p. 5).[13] He concludes his chapter by noting the dire consequences for any society comprised of men and women who take to heart the teachings of *The Green Book*. The very qualities that civilization most requires are vitiated by the teaching of Gaius and Titius.

Lewis took these consequences seriously, and was even more biting in private than he was in public. In a letter to Martyn Skinner written only a few days after he delivered the lectures that become *Abolition*, Lewis answered Skinner's question about the relationship between Christianity and the *Tao*:

> The relation between the Tao and Xtianity is best seen from Confucius' remark "There may be someone who has perfectly followed the way: but I never heard of one." Gaius and Titius were, as you will not be surprised to learn, Australians. Singapore knows what comes of Green Books now.
>
> Lewis, 2004, p. 561[14]

The reference to Singapore strikes a modern audience as obscure but would have had an immediate meaning to a British reader in 1943. The Fall of Singapore in February 1942 was a monumental disaster for British morale overall and British strategy in the Pacific. While accounts of the battle vary, the British public widely believed that much of the blame lay with thousands of undertrained Australian troops who abandoned their posts and fled the scene. Lewis is making a direct (and perhaps not entirely fair) link between the teachings of Gaius and Titius and the putative cowardice of the Australian troops.

"We make men without chests and expected of them virtue and enterprise" (2001a, p. 27), Lewis writes near the end of this first chapter, and it is on the battlefield that we will see this outcome most tragically illustrated. It is not a surprise that Lewis, the wounded veteran who served in the trenches of the First World War, makes dying in battle for one's country a key piece of his treatment of *The Green Book*. There is a reason Lewis sums up the import of the first lecture with his first sentence of the second lecture, "The practical result of education in the spirit of *The Green Book* must be the destruction of the society which accepts it."[15] We see here illustrated one of the traditional concerns of natural law theory in that the health and flourishing of any society depends on the moral education of its citizens. Lewis' approach in the first lecture reveals not only the importance of natural law for society, but also an understanding of human nature.

Lewis could be so concerned about the impact of a grade school textbook because he subscribed to a Platonic view of the person and an Aristotelian approach to education. Plato's *Republic* uses the analogy of the well-ordered city to illustrate the well-ordered soul. In Plato's hypothetical city, justice is achieved when the different classes of the city mind their own business, wise philosophers, courageous auxiliaries, and moderate workers doing their part to make the city work. Likewise, the human being is well ordered when the reasonable mind allies with the well-trained emotions of the heart to regulate the desires of the stomach.[16]

Lewis agreed with Plato and Aristotle (and John Locke) that the training of emotions must begin even before the mind is developed enough to engage in abstract rational thought. The child must be taught to respond correctly to this or that situation so that when she is old enough to *think* about morality, she will already have the grooves set in her moral character to accept what reason teaches. This is why Lewis is at pains to emphasize that certain realities in the world objectively merit certain types of reactions, and why he debunks Gaius and Titius's debunking of emotions.

For example, Lewis identifies "duties to parents, elders, and ancestors" as a branch of the first principle of special beneficence, and offers several examples from his collection of sources. "I tended the old man, I gave him my staff," Lewis quotes from an ancient Egyptian source (2001a, p. 91). We can imagine a young boy walking with his father and older brothers and witnessing an older man tripping on the side of the road. If the father and brothers laugh at the man, the young boy will learn the wrong lesson by example and by joining in. The world is such that an older person falling down *merits* a compassionate response, just as a magnificent waterfall can somehow rightly elicit our awe. The proper emotional response is compassion, and the proper action to undertake is to help the old man. When he is older the boy may learn the right thing to do, but he will be much more likely to do it if his emotions have been properly trained from the start. "Without the aid of the trained emotions," Lewis writes, "the intellect is powerless against the animal organism" (2001a, p. 24).

This example also connects well with the Aristotelian emphasis on learning by doing. Both Plato and Aristotle teach the importance of example, but Aristotle in particular teaches that our character is not only formed by our examples but by what we do. In some ways, what we do can be even more important than what we are taught cognitively, as we see in Lewis' statement that he'd rather play cards with a man skeptical about objective morality but raised to think that cheating was wrong, than the impeccably credentialed moral philosopher who was raised by con men.

Lewis' first lecture accomplishes three things. First, he draws connections between children's education, natural law teaching, and the health and even survival of civilization. As mentioned above, natural law has real life applications and outcomes. Second, he stakes out a position on human nature and education. Human beings are rational, emotional, and desiring creatures, whose wellbeing depends on the proper ordering of those elements of the soul. They learn by example and by repetition of virtuous acts. Any effective understanding of natural law that ignores or contradicts these truths works against the grain of human nature. Finally, he exposes the false pretenses of Gaius and Titius's pedagogy and sets the stage for an even more devastating review of them in the subsequent chapter.

"The Way"

One of the most intriguing features of *Abolition* is how Lewis frames the debate. Many works of natural law theory assume a defensive position. That is, the author assumes that natural law is in the dock and must be proved valid or reasonable. Lewis doesn't take this tack. Indeed, one of the most enjoyable aspects of *Abolition* is how he turns the tables. Instead of assuming that the *Tao* must be established or defended, he proposes to interrogate the alternatives. Gaius and Titius aim to undermine the old values by teaching students to "see through" old-fashioned sentiments and moral judgments. Why should we think it's up to us to defend our position? Rather, what motivates them? And what do they propose as a replacement?

Lewis begins his treatment of Gaius and Titius's philosophy by pressing them on these very questions, noting that their very act of writing the book indicates they think it will serve some purpose (2001a, pp. 28–29). What sort of purpose? Lewis' contention is that the authors of *The Green Book* must, at some point, admit that they seek to produce in their students some appreciation of a value that is good for its own sake. He does this by treating any number of alternative motivations to good *qua* good. But every alternative leads back to reliance on some good for its own sake. Efficiency, utility, and progress all raise the question of "to what end?"[17] And "instinct" turns out to be an incoherent explanation for how we can be morally obligated to do what various and competing instincts might be telling us to do.

Lewis does more than pick apart a side here, however. He endorses the reality of the natural law, or the *Tao*, or the dictates or practical reason, by a process of elimination. Given that Gaius and Titius do have real values they are trying to inculcate into school children, and given there is no way to ground those values in anything more fundamental than their intrinsic goodness, natural law is not one option among many but the "sole source of all value judgments." Every value that Gaius or Titius might want to preserve while jettisoning older traditional values still leads them back to what is and can only be intrinsically good.[18] That is, it leads them back to the *Tao*. And this is a victory for Lewis even if they want to quibble with whether this or that value belongs in the *Tao*. This is because Lewis is not trying to establish all the contours of a viable natural law *theory*. He is trying to reawaken his readers to the reality of the natural law itself. Lewis admits that we shall find "many contradictions and absurdities" if we try to reconcile all the sources and various traditions that offer witness to the *Tao* (2001a, p. 45). But if Gaius and Titius are forced to explain why posterity or economic success are goods (pp. 43–44) and some other good is not, they are back in the arena of objective morality. If their preferred value really is good, by what rule can they exclude those they have been debunking?[19]

Lewis' argument here does address one important natural law theory controversy, and that is how to think about the is/ought question. For Lewis plants himself squarely in the camp of those natural lawyers who do not believe moral norms can be deduced from facts about human nature. "From propositions about fact alone no *practical* conclusion can ever be drawn" (2001a, p. 31). As such, practical conclusions can only follow from practical premises, and self-evident or basic premises at that. In theoretical reason we cannot ask for proof of the principle of non-contradiction, nor in mathematical reasoning can we ask for the proof by which we can ascertain the transitive principle that if A equals B, and B equal C, then A equals C.

So it is with practical reasoning. "You must not hold a pistol to the head of the *Tao*," Lewis writes, and in this insistence on the basic nature of moral precepts we have an important key to characterizing the thrust of this middle chapter. "The Way" is an extended meditation on the truth of the first principle of practical reason. That principle, as articulated by Thomas Aquinas, is to do good and avoid evil.[20] There is no response to be made to someone who asks why we should favor good rather than evil, no more fundamental ground to appeal to. As it is with this first principle, so it is, Lewis claims, with all the other tenets of the *Tao* that we see in the major headings of the appendix. What is perhaps most clever about this chapter is Lewis' attempt to co-opt Gaius and Titius and any reader who wishes to maintain a genuine commitment to the objectivity of this or that moral good. Does racism violate a truly objective and knowable moral principle? Or is anti-racism merely a subjective taboo that some societies have happened upon at this particular juncture of human history? What about domestic violence? Or a callous disregard for the environment? Slavery?

To think that any of these things is objectively wrong across time and culture as opposed to the idiosyncratic and transitory commitment of a given society reveals a belief in certain goods genuinely constitutive of human nature such that these evils can violate them. As we have seen over and over, Lewis' strategy is not one of establishing what's right by argument. It is, rather, an endeavor to wake his readers up by appealing to what they already tacitly know is right. It is an attempt to let the light of the *Tao*'s intrinsic reasonableness shine not by producing the light itself but by exposing the ethereal flimsiness of the shadowy alternatives.

"The Abolition of Man"?

Lewis' argument in his concluding chapter clearly reveals the chasm between two radically different and incommensurable positions. There are those who accept the *Tao* or even some shred of it as intrinsically valuable on the one side, and there are those like Nietzsche and his ideological children who hasten to welcome a post-human future. We should note that Gaius and Titius and those like them fall on one side of the divide, Lewis' side. It is because Lewis thinks they actually are trying—albeit in a truncated way—to advance real moral values that Lewis can portray them as holding onto scraps of the *Tao* and recall them to their humanity.

There is no such recourse with Nietzsche. Lewis' warning in this last chapter is that putting human nature itself under the reductionist microscope is to cross an unprecedented boundary. Who, or rather what, would be looking through the microscope? We need not rehearse Lewis' full line of reasoning here. His logic appears to be irresistible. If human nature, human purpose, and the moral virtues needed to fulfill that purpose are not givens but projects to be created by existing human beings, the soon-to-be obsolete morality has no authoritative claim to guide the choices of the conditioners. This may be a grave concern to those of us who accept the authority of natural law. It will be a welcome development for Nietzsche and his last men.

What Lewis saw as an impending future we can now see as part of our present. Lewis' warning was explicitly welcomed by the behavioral psychologist B.F. Skinner, who considered Lewis' book in his 1971 Nietzschean-titled offering *Beyond Freedom and Dignity*. Skinner is the precursor of what is today an even more widespread movement of transhumanists and posthumanists. His reaction to Lewis' warning about abolishing human nature is worth quoting at length:

> What is being abolished is autonomous man—the inner man, the homunculus, the possessing demon, the man defended by the literatures of freedom and dignity.
>
> His abolition has long been overdue. Autonomous man is a device used to explain what we cannot explain in any other way. He has been constructed by our ignorance, and as our understanding increases, the very stuff of which he is composed vanishes. Science does not dehumanize man, it de-homunculizes him, and it must do so if it is to prevent the abolition of the human species. To man *qua* man we readily say good riddance. Only by dispossessing him can we turn to the real causes of human behavior. Only then can we turn from the inferred to the observed, from the miraculous to the natural, from the inaccessible to the manipulable.
>
> Skinner, 1971, p. 200

While Skinner seems to think he is responding to Lewis' argument, he's actually restating it. Lewis might press Skinner on what he means by "overdue," or "the natural," or what informs the relief with which we say good riddance to man as he once was. Yet the only real difference between the two of them is that Skinner welcomes the abolition, and Lewis warns us against it.

Lewis encountered an earlier version of Skinnerism in his own college. While Lewis was eating with a friend at the university, a rector and philosopher named Marett joined them, touting news of a mid-century version of simian viagra:

"I saw in the papers this morning that there is some scientist fellow in Vienna, called Voronoff—some name like that—who has invented a way of splicing the glands of young apes onto old gentlemen, thereby renewing their generative powers! Remarkable, isn't it?"

Lewis thought.

"*I would say 'unnatural.'*"

"Come, come! 'Unnatural!' What do you mean 'unnatural?' Voronoff is a part of Nature, isn't he? What happens in Nature must surely be natural? Speaking as a philosopher, don't you know"—(Marett taught Philosophy)—"I can attach no meaning to your objection; I don't understand you!"

"*I am sorry, Rector; but I think any philosopher from Aristotle to—say—Jeremy Bentham, would have understood me.*"

"Oh well, we've got beyond Bentham by now, I hope. If Aristotle or he had known about Voronoff, they might have changed their ideas. Think of the possibilities he opens up! You'll be an old man yourself one day."

"*I would rather be an old man than a young monkey.*"

Meilander, 1978, p. 184

What else is there to say to the Maretts and Skinners of the world? If Lewis is correct, there is no argument that can reach their lack of grounded presuppositions. We come back full circle to the Dwarfs depicted in *The Last Battle* or the characters of Lewis' fictionalized version of *Abolition* in *That Hideous Strength*.[21] The best we can hope for on an argumentative level is laying out the two sides with as much rigor and accuracy as possible. As far the positions go, there is no digging deep enough to find a common foundation.

But is that all there is to say for Lewis' apologetics on behalf of the natural law? I have argued already that Lewis' masterwork on the natural law leaves out many aspects of natural law that usually accompany natural law theories. Yet we should not fault Lewis for failing to accomplish what he did not set out to do. We would need to go elsewhere in his writings to find more details about politics and natural law application, and about humanity's ultimate purpose.[22] We do find in *Abolition* Lewis describing something of the architecture of practical reason, both with regard to the nature of human beings and our capacity to apprehend first principles, and also with regard to what Lewis called the "primeval moral platitudes" and some of their most immediate applications. Lewis also paints a vivid picture through the three lectures of what is at stake for not only particular societies but the human race. How one reacts to that vivid picture depends, Lewis would tell us, on how well we have been trained in the *Tao*.

Would Lewis tell us that those who reject the *Tao* are unreachable? If we think only of the argumentative plane, then Lewis' answer is "yes." The differences between the positions go that deep. But *Abolition* and Lewis' other works are not addressed to positions. They are addressed to people, and as Lewis notes in an endnote regarding a Skinner-like professor named C.H. Waddington, sometimes people's hearts are better than the theories in their heads (Lewis, 2001a, p. 108). For while the positions may be incommensurable, there is still some hope that those who try to entirely reject the *Tao* still bear the imprint of their Maker, the *imago dei*.[23]

While the arguments may be incommensurable, we cannot know for certain that those who reject the *Tao* are unreachable. In another essay regarding how to make the positive case for Christianity, Lewis gives us another way to understand what he's up to with his negative case against moral nihilism in *Abolition*. In "The Grand Miracle," Lewis is considering how to weigh the evidence for the Incarnation, a singular event so improbable that there is no regular standard of proof that could be brought in to feasibly gauge its historicity. What can be done if there's no common ground upon which to have an argument? One must apply a different standard:

> Supposing you had before you a manuscript of some great work, either a symphony or a novel. There then comes to you a person, saying "Here is a new bit of the manuscript that I found; it is the central passage of that symphony, or the central chapter of that novel. The text is incomplete without it. I have got the missing passage which is really the centre of the whole work." The only thing you could do would be to put this new piece of the manuscript in that central position, and then see how it reacted on the whole of the rest of the work. If it constantly brought out new meanings . . ., if it made you notice things . . . which you had not noticed before, then I think you would decide it was authentic. On the other hand, if it failed to do that, then, however attractive it was in itself, you would reject it.
>
> Lewis, 1989, p. 81

Lewis takes this standard of "fit" and argues that the Incarnation works just in this way with regard to human experience. I am suggesting that the stark portrayal of the conditioners in *Abolition* and in Lewis' fiction is meant to act as the negative version of the Incarnation in Lewis' hypothetical symphony and novel. Lewis' accomplishment in *Abolition* is to so powerfully portray the alternative to natural law thinking that when we try to make sense of a post-human "morality," we will have the eyes to *see* that such a conception makes nonsense of everything we already know, believe, and treasure about the good, the true, and the beautiful.

Lewis' *Abolition* is an anti-gospel, a jarring anti-Incarnational vision depicting not God becoming man but man tearing out of himself—if it is possible—the very nature given to him by God. That is the message that Lewis the natural law apologist would have us communicate to a world increasingly deaf and blind to the power of practical reason and the basic nature of moral reality. It does not provide us with every answer that we might want from a natural law theory, but its power lies in its witness to the reality of an enduring human nature governed by foundational moral precepts, and the stark unveiling of what the alternative to the *Tao* truly means.

Notes

1 See also "Modern Man and his Categories of Thought" (Lewis, 1986, pp. 61–66).

2 Some of this thinking here is indebted to my previous work on this topic (Watson, 2013, pp. 200–201).

3 An important note here is that while natural law theories can become more or less influential in a culture, natural law itself does not wax or wane. Natural law is a reality irrespective of how widely accepted it happens to be in a particular time or place (Finnis, 1980, p. 24).

4 See *Summa Theologica* I–II 91 (Aquinas, 1998, p. 46) Thomas also brings in epistemology here in how he distinguishes natural law from eternal law. That is, the difference between natural law and eternal law is not substantive in content. All of natural law is eternal law. The difference is how human beings know or access it.

5 Lewis addresses the thorny question of God's relationship to the moral law in what is effectively a companion piece to *Abolition*, "The Poison of Subjectivism" (Lewis, 1967). ("On Ethics" in the same volume is another companion piece.) Here he considers the Euthyphro dilemma, which asks whether the moral law's goodness comes from God's willing it to be so, or whether God promulgates the moral law because it is good. Lewis also tackles this problem with the help of the Anglican

philosopher Richard Hooker in his *English Literature in the Sixteenth Century Excluding Drama* (Lewis, 1954, p. 49).

6 "In order to avoid misunderstanding, I may add that though I myself am a Theist, and indeed a Christian, I am not here attempting any indirect argument for Theism" (Lewis, 2001a, p. 49).

7 This is not to say that Lewis or other natural law proponents think that human beings can achieve their purpose of eternal fellowship with God by doing good deeds and avoiding evil.

8 See, for instance, Finnis *et al.* (1987) and Tollefsen (2014).

9 It may be helpful to remember Lewis' analogy of the ships and intra-ship morality is not the same thing as where the ships are going (Lewis, 1960, p. 56–57).

10 "For Thou hast made us for Thyself and our hearts are restless till they rest in Thee" (Augustine, 1993, p. 3). From the Westminster Shorter Catechism, "Q. 1. *What is the chief end of man?* A. Man"s chief end is to glorify God, and to enjoy him forever" (Rohls, 1998, 65). C.S. Lewis, "First and Second Things," in *God in the Dock* (Lewis, 1989), and *Mere Christianity* (Lewis, 1960, p. 39).

11 "This chapter, then, is an invitation to reflect on one form of human activity, the activity of trying to find out, to understand, and to judge matters correctly. This is not, perhaps, the easiest activity to understand; but it has the advantage of being the activity which the reader himself is actually engaged in" (Finnis, 1980, pp. 60–61).

12 "So he sent the word to slay And slew the little childer" (Lewis, 2001a, p. 1).

13 Lewis anticipates the work of his one-time debating partner G.E.M. Anscombe's trenchant critique in "Modern Moral Philosophy" (1958) and Alasdair MacIntyre's masterwork *After Virtue* (1981).

14 Whether this was fair to Australians or not, it still gives us some insight into Lewis' thinking about the authors.

15 Lewis does not fill in the missing elements to this argument here, but his "Why I am not a Pacifist" essay does (Lewis, 2001b).

16 See, for example, *The Republic of Plato* (Plato, 1991, pp. 261–262). Lewis cites Plato directly in *Abolition* (Lewis, 2001a, p. 24).

17 Even the great philosopher of utilitarianism, John Stuart Mill, envisioned utility as "grounded on the permanent interests of man as a progressive being" (Mill, 2006, p. 17).

18 For Lewis' description of the goods Gaius and Titius have in mind, we must look to his first endnote on page 105.

19 Lewis had made this move before in *The Pilgrim's Regress*. In the first book Lewis wrote after becoming a Christian, the lady Reason slays the Spirit of the Age with three questions, the second of which anticipates the bind Lewis puts Gaius and Titius in:

> Now hear my second riddle. There was a certain man who was going to his own house and his enemy went with him. And his house was beyond a river too swift to swim and too deep to wade. And he could go no faster than his enemy. While he was on his journey his wife sent to him and said, "You know that there is only one bridge across the river: tell me, shall I destroy it that the enemy may not cross; or shall I leave it standing that you may cross? What shall this man do?"
>
> Lewis, 2014, p. 56

20 I am not saying that Lewis intended this as a commentary on Thomas in particular. Lewis was not a Thomistic scholar. I'm saying he's pointing to the same thing that Thomas pointed to.

21 See Chapter X in this volume.

22 For more on Lewis' politics and the natural law generally, see Dyer and Watson (2016).

23 Granted, Lewis does say that the conditioners will no longer be men, having given up what truly makes them human. Whether Lewis truly thought this was entirely possible is debatable. His speculation about damned souls visiting Heaven in *The Great Divorce* is suggestive, as is Lucy's wondering in *Prince Caspian* whether people could lose their souls as talking animals in Narnia had: "Wouldn't it be dreadful if some day in our own world at home, men started going wild inside, like the animals here, and still looked like men, so that you'd never know which were which?" (Lewis, 1979, p. 128).

Works cited

Anscombe, G.E.M. (1958), "Modern Moral Philosophy," *Philosophy*, 33 (124), 1–19.

Aquinas, Thomas (1998), *St. Thomas on Politics and Ethics* (ed. and trans. Paul E. Sigmund). New York: W.W. Norton & Company.

Aristotle (1987), *The Nicomachean Ethics* (trans. D. Ross). Oxford: Oxford University Press.

Augustine (1993), *Confessions* (trans. F.J. Sheed). Indianapolis, IN: Hackett.

Dyer, J. and Watson, M. (2016), *C.S. Lewis on Politics and the Natural Law*. Cambridge: Cambridge University Press.

Finnis, J. (1980), *Natural Law and Natural Rights*. Oxford: Oxford University Press.

Finnis, J., Boyle, J.M., Jr. and Grisez, G. (1987), *Nuclear Deterrence, Morality, and Realism*. Oxford: Clarendon Press.

Lewis, C.S. (1946), *The Great Divorce*. New York: Macmillan.

Lewis, C.S. (1954), *English Literature in the Sixteenth Century Excluding Drama*. New York: Oxford University Press.

Lewis, C.S. (1960), *Mere Christianity*. New York: Macmillan.
Lewis, C.S. (1967), *Christian Reflections* (ed. W. Hooper). Grand Rapids, MI: Eerdmans.
Lewis, C.S. (1978), *Miracles*. New York: Macmillan.
Lewis, C.S. (1979), *Prince Caspian*. New York: HarperCollins.
Lewis, C.S. (1984), *The Last Battle*. New York: HarperCollins.
Lewis, C.S. (1986), "Modern Man and his Categories of Thought," in *Present Concerns*. San Diego, CA: Harcourt Brace Jovanovich.
Lewis, C.S. (1989), *God in the Dock* (ed. W. Hooper). Grand Rapids, MI: Eerdmans.
Lewis, C.S. (1996a), *Perelandra*. New York: Scribner.
Lewis, C.S. (1996b), *The Screwtape Letters*. New York: HarperCollins.
Lewis, C.S. (2001a), *The Abolition of Man*. New York: HarperCollins.
Lewis, C.S. (2001b), *The Weight of Glory*. New York: HarperCollins.
Lewis, C.S. (2004), *The Collected Letters of C.S. Lewis*, Vol. II (ed. W. Hooper). New York: HarperCollins.
Lewis, C.S. (2014), *The Pilgrim's Regress* (ed. D.C. Downing). Grand Rapids, MI: Eerdmans.
MacIntyre, A. (1981), *After Virtue: A Study in Moral Theory*. London: Duckworth.
Meilander, G. (1978), *The Taste for the Other: The Social and Ethical Thought of C.S. Lewis*. Grand Rapids, MI: Eerdmans.
Mill, J.S. (2006), *On Liberty and the Subjection of Women* (ed. A. Ryan). New York: Penguin Classics.
Plato (1991), *The Republic of Plato* (2nd edn., ed. A. Bloom). New York, NY: Basic Books.
Rohls, Jan (1998), *Reformed Confessions: From Zurich to Barmen*. Louisville, KY: Westminster John Knox Press.
Skinner, B.F. (1971), *Beyond Freedom and Dignity*. Indianapolis, IN: Hackett.
Tollefsen, C.O. (2014), *Lying and Christian Ethics*. Cambridge: Cambridge University Press.
Watson, M. (2013), "C.S. Lewis as natural law evangelist: Evangelical political thought and the people in the pew," in J. Covington, B. McGraw and M. Watson (eds.), *Natural Law and Evangelical Political Thought*. Lanham, MD: Lexington Books, pp. 195–224.

3

Education in *The Abolition of Man*

Mark Pike
University of Leeds

C.S. Lewis is recognized as a literary author, a scholar of English literature, and as perhaps the twentieth-century's greatest Christian apologist but he is not generally recognized as an educator. Most books with titles like *The Great Educators* generally include chapters on key figures in education. One chapter is usually devoted to Plato, one to Rousseau, even perhaps one to Milton and certainly one to Dewey, but such books are unlikely to include the name of C.S. Lewis. Despite this neglect, my contention is that C.S. Lewis is one of the truly great educators and that his thought on education and schooling is highly relevant today (Pike, 2013).

This is easy to miss because there is no one "big book" on education and schooling by C.S. Lewis and *The Abolition of Man* is a very "small book" (originally with only 64 pages). As the thought of C.S. Lewis on education and schooling is liberally distributed across his fiction, literary criticism, theology and ethics, one of the aims of *Mere Education—C.S. Lewis as Teacher for our Time* (Pike, 2013) was to draw this material together and synthesize it in one volume for educators. This is significant because the thought of C.S. Lewis enables us to see clearly and challenge assumptions about many widely accepted educational beliefs and practices that are often taken for granted in our time (Pike, 2012). Across the Lewis canon we find remarkably prescient insights and ethical analysis of educational issues and practices in pedagogy, curriculum and instruction, student–teacher dialogue, logical reasoning, reading, task design, marking and grading, formative and summative assessment, work ethic, equality and rights in education, sex and relationships education, democratic education, educational leadership, discipline, behavior management, and character education (the list goes on).

The Abolition of Man is important not because it deals with the full range of specific educational practices (which Lewis addresses elsewhere) but because it deals with the foundations of education and schooling that are especially important for teachers and school leaders. Indeed, the three parts of *The Abolition of Man* were originally given as lectures to school teachers, and its subtitle is *Reflections on education with special reference to the teaching of English in the upper forms of schools*. The significance of *The Abolition of Man* in the twenty-first century lies not only in the insights it offers about the nature and purpose of schooling, but also in its "prophetic" understanding. C.S. Lewis is remarkably prescient about the direction of culture and society (in which schooling is located) and the sort of issues with which we would have to deal. It is here in *The Abolition of Man* that C.S. Lewis defines the "task of the modern educator" being "to irrigate deserts" by which he means it is "to inculcate just sentiments" (Lewis, 1978, p. 14). This chapter seeks to provide an analysis of these "deserts" and how they might be "irrigated."

The education of character: Objective value

The first part of *The Abolition of Man* is entitled "Men Without Chests" because the heads (the intellect) of the students look bigger than their chests (their character). Lewis shows that each of us is more than an intellect (a head) and more than an animal with appetite (a stomach) for we have a moral sense and character (a chest). We should remember that Lewis is describing the "graduate" of the schooling system he observed. If this was a cartoon character, it would be the opposite of the "bodybuilder" with an expanded chest and small head. The schooling system Lewis saw produced young people whose chest (their character) was atrophied through lack of exercise. His assessment was not that schooling had educated the head (the intellect) too much but that it had educated the chest (character) too little. The reason for this neglect was that there was no acceptance of objective truth, the necessary equipment upon which to exercise the chest (good character).

C.S. Lewis illustrates this with reference to one of the books for schools he had just reviewed. He makes the point that textbooks for schools such as *The Green Book* and teachers like Gaius and Titius (its authors) may do education and schooling more than a disservice; they are dangerous because they are indoctrinatory (in the pejorative sense) and teach unsuspecting students a falsehood, that values are relative. The values inculcated by the book are so potent because they are latent. Lewis discerns clear "Approvals" and "Disapprovals" in the "real (perhaps unconscious) philosophy" of its authors who reflect the "whole system of values which happened to be in vogue" at the time of writing (1978, p. 38).

The student has no notion that "ethics, theology, and politics are all at stake" and this is an abuse of power because the student "cannot know what is being done to him" (Lewis, 1978, p. 9). Lewis' verdict, with regard to the impact on the student, is that the book's authors, "while teaching him nothing about letters, have cut out his soul, long before he is old enough to choose" (p. 11). Cutting out the soul results in the atrophy of the chest, especially when the excision is before the learner is "old enough to choose."

The relativism Lewis objects to so vehemently is apparent in the way *The Green Book* presents the well-known incident in literary history of the Romantic poet Coleridge at the waterfall, Cora Linn, in Scotland. Coleridge meets two tourists; one describes the waterfall as "sublime" and the other considers it to be "pretty" or "beautiful." Coleridge (and Lewis) recognize the accuracy of the former description and the error of the latter. The "sublime" is definitely not "pretty." This is not an obscure literary point nor is it about Coleridge being pedantic. Longinus (1964) shows us that the "sublime" is that which inspires awe; Burke (1958) notes the sublime inspires terror as well as awe; and Kant (1974) explains that what is so terrifying about the "sublime" is that it has no boundaries. Lewis explains that "certain responses can be more 'just' or 'ordinate' than others" (1978, p. 14). This is a foundational point: there is a right response and a wrong response by human beings to aspects of the world around them. C.S. Lewis declares that "emotions and sentiments . . . can be reasonable or unreasonable as they conform to Reason or fail to conform" (p. 16). What made Lewis so concerned about this textbook for schools was the emphasis upon the *subjectivity* of the reader: "The man who called the cataract sublime was not intending simply to describe his own emotions about it: he was also claiming that the object was one which *merited* those emotions" (p. 14).

There is a right relation and a wrong relation between human beings and certain acts, events, and situations we come across during our studies and in life. Lewis explains that certain responses in life really are better than others. What he defends can be summed up as:

> . . . the doctrine of objective value, the belief that certain attitudes are really true, and others really false, to the kind of thing the universe is and the kind of things we are.
>
> 1978, p. 16

There is, however, a gulf between this classical view and modern values talk: "We moderns are apt to say that something is good because we value it, a crucial and highly problematic reversal of the idea found in the ancients that we cherish something because of its goodness" (Higgins, 2010, p. 221). Similarly, Lewis reminds us:

> Until quite modern times all teachers and even all men believed . . . that objects did not merely receive, but could *merit*, our approval or disapproval, our reverence or contempt.
>
> 1978, p. 14

The rise of moral relativism has had a profound influence. If students do not ask "Is it true?" or "Is it right?" and instead ask "Is it my truth?" or "Does it feel right for me?," then education will not be worth the name. In Latin, *educatio* signifies what we now refer to as "bringing up" children. Jean Bethke Elshtain recalls her daughter being taught, in the fifth grade, in a school in a New England college town, that values were simply "subjective opinions"; she asked her daughter if slavery was "wrong" and the response was "I think slavery is wrong . . . but that is just my opinion" (Elshtain, 2008, p. 88). The danger of such teaching is that it undermines our humanity and militates against human dignity; it leads to the abolition of man, the termination of our humanity. Moral relativism and subjectivism make it impossible to educate for good character. College professor Christina Hoff-Sommers (1985) came to that conclusion when she tried to find an act that her first-year philosophy students would universally condemn as morally wrong: "Torturing a child, starving someone to death, humiliating an invalid in a nursing home. Their reply is often, 'torture, starvation, and humiliation may be bad for you or for me, but who are we to say they are bad for someone else?'" (Hoff-Sommers, 1985, p. 164). It is significant that, "Many of our youth do not understand or accept absolute truth—that is, that which is true for all people, for all times, for all places" (McDowell and Hostetler, 1994, p. 17).

What Lewis objected to was a textbook for schools promoting the general philosophical theory that all values are subjective, which could then result in students holding views such as these. We now know that *The Green Book* was King and Ketley's *The Control of Language* (1939) and when I visited the Wade Center to research *Mere Education* I was privileged to read the annotations Lewis had made in his personal copy. He had underlined as follows: "'The difficulty of thinking and writing about idealism and ideals is that these words *do not stand for anything definite*" (King and Ketley, 1939, p. 92).[1] The retort in his handwritten annotation was: "They do when I use 'em!" (unpublished material, p. 92 in C. S. Lewis' hand, my italics).[2]

The education of character: Universal virtues

C.S. Lewis shows that "objective value" is at the core of what it is to be a human being. It is also vital if we are to develop the constellation of universal virtues that underpin good character. Acknowledging that morality stands outside of us and must be independent of our subjectivities is vital because, as Lewis pointed out, "the judge cannot be one of the parties judged" (1978, p. 28). If one does not recognize objective truth, one has no basis or foundation upon which to cultivate virtue.

"The Way" is the title of the second part of *The Abolition of Man* where Lewis explains that the basis for the development of virtue based on objective truth is the Moral Law or what he calls the *Tao* (pronounced *Dao*). The *Tao* is "Nature, it is the Way, the Road" (Lewis, 1978, p. 15). Lewis states that "this conception in all its forms, Platonic, Aristotelian, Stoic, Christian, and Oriental alike, I shall henceforth refer to for brevity simply as 'the *Tao*'" (1978, p. 16). Lewis uses terms such as "righteousness," "correctness," "order," and "truth" to denote the *Tao* (p. 15), which is innate and universal. Lewis acknowledges "though I myself am a Theist, and indeed a Christian, I am not here attempting any indirect argument for Theism ... Whether [there is] a supernatural origin for the *Tao* is a question I am not here concerned with" (p. 32). Of course, St. Paul wrote of a natural moral law written on the human heart that enables us to know right from wrong. Significantly, at the same time that Paul was writing that those who are not Jews "show the work of the law written in their hearts" (Romans 2.15), the Roman statesman Cicero was writing that there is a "true law" that is "unchangeable and eternal" (*De Republica*, 11.33). Of course, we need to be clear that in *The Abolition of Man* Lewis is not articulating a specifically Christian morality, although he does so elsewhere (Lewis, 1981; see Pike, 2013, 2014). C.S. Lewis explains that what he has "called for convenience the Tao" others may call "Natural Law" (1978, p. 33). In the *Summa Theologica*, St. Thomas Aquinas states that within Natural Law there are "first, certain most general precepts, that are known to all; and secondly, certain secondary and more detailed precepts, which are, as it were, conclusions following closely from first principles" and states that the secondary precepts of the Natural Law "can be blotted out from the human heart, either by evil persuasions . . . or by vicious customs and corrupt habits . . . and even unnatural vices" (Aquinas, I–II. Q96. A6).

The Abolition of Man is valuable because it shows how the religious and literary texts of a range of cultures (as diverse as the ancient Egyptian, Babylonian, Old Norse, Chinese, Indian, Jewish, Roman, Greek, Australian Aboriginal, and American Indian) underpin the *Tao*. Lewis gives "illustrations of the Natural Law" (1978 p. 56) in eight "laws." The first law of "General Beneficence" is summed up as "Refrain from murder or bringing any sort of misery and suffering upon one's fellows; love others as oneself." The second law of "Special Beneficence" instructs us to "Fulfil the special duties we have to family or subjects." The third law concerns "Duties to Parents, Elders, Ancestors." The fourth law of the *Tao* relates to "Duties to Children and Posterity" and requires us to provide for the education of the young and to respect children. The fifth law is that of Justice and might be summed up as "Be faithful to one's spouse. Do not steal; render to each person his rights. The legal system should not be partial and treat the poor worse than the rich." The sixth law is that of "Good Faith and Veracity," which proscribes lies and fraud and requires the keeping of promises. The seventh law of "Mercy" requires us to "Care for the weak—the poor, the sick, the disabled, widows, orphans, and the elderly." The eighth law is that of "Magnanimity" where we are commanded, "Do not injure; protect others from being injured."

We find expressions of the *Tao* throughout schooling but increasingly, in children's reading for instance, we are seeing the increasing popularity of many books that do not support traditional morality (Pike, 2015). This is in contrast to the Narnia novels, which are "part of the great moral tradition of humankind, that Lewis in *The Abolition of Man* calls the *Tao*" (Tankard, 2007, p. 72). Taking opportunities for "teaching the *Tao*" are important and recently the "Narnian Virtues" curriculum has sought to do just that. Twelve virtues (wisdom, love, fortitude, courage, self-control, justice, forgiveness, gratitude, humility, integrity, hard work, and curiosity) that are universally applicable are learned by students with a variety of social, cultural, and religious backgrounds as they engage with the Narnia novels (Pike *et al.*, 2015). Findings confirm the view of literary critic, Laura Miller, who argues in *The Magician's Book—A Sceptic's Adventures in Narnia* (2008), that far from being the work of an exclusively Christian author, Lewis' Narnia novels are for all of us. Clearly, Lewis' *Tao* is foundational for schooling because only when we operate "within the *Tao*" is there the possibility of virtues (such as self-control):

> While we speak from within the *Tao* we can speak of Man having power over himself in a sense truly analogous to an individual's self-control. But the moment we step outside and regard the *Tao* as a mere subjective product, this possibility has disappeared.
>
> Lewis, 1978, p. 51

The entire educational project is fundamentally altered by one's beliefs about the *Tao* (or the existence of objective Natural Law that compels our allegiance). Once we accept this foundation, we need to "train" our students (even though "training" in the sense of inculcation may sound old-fashioned to some twenty-first century ears):

> Hence the educational problem is wholly different according as you stand within or without the *Tao*. For those within, the task is *to train in the pupil* those responses which are in themselves appropriate, whether anyone is making them or not, and in making which the very nature of man consists.
>
> Lewis, 1978, p. 17, my italics

The education of character: Training in virtue

Lewis acknowledges that "no justification of virtue will enable a man to be virtuous" (1978, p. 20). We need "training" as "we will not at first have the right responses" and "must be *trained* to feel pleasure, liking, disgust, and hatred at those things which really are pleasant, likeable, disgusting and hateful" (p. 15, my italics). The importance of "trained emotions" (p. 20) is of determining significance for the cultivation of virtue.

C.S. Lewis shows us in *The Abolition of Man* that schooling often fails to nurture the moral character of students or the "chest", which is the seat "of emotions organized by *trained habit* into stable sentiments" (1978, p. 19, my italics). These "sentiments" are important to education in the virtues. In Lewis' own copy of *The Abolition of Man*, in the archive at the Wade Center, which he sent to his former Philosophy tutor, E.F. Carritt, he added the annotation that "a right code of conduct is 'more easily obeyed if our passions are *trained* to add their weight'" (unpublished material, p. 14 in C.S. Lewis' hand, my italics).[3]

Clearly, the premise of neo-Aristotelian-inspired character education is that the more you practise virtue the better you get, and Lewis appears here every bit the "character educator." Indeed, "in its underlying philosophy, character education rejects moral relativism and reasserts the idea of moral objectivity" (Lickona, 1996, p. 299), which, as we have seen, is what Lewis does in the first part of *The Abolition of Man*. Furthermore, Berkowitz and Bier (2004) have pointed out that character education "has long relied upon an Aristotelian principle that character is formed in large part through habitual behaviour that eventually becomes internalized into virtues" (p. 80), and in *The Abolition of Man* Lewis approvingly refers to Aristotle's view that, "the aim of education is to make the pupil like and dislike what he ought" (1978, p. 14).

At this point, Lewis could be accused, as character education has been accused, of a crude behaviorism. For instance, Kohn (1997), a prominent critic of character education, charged that it was "behaviorist," seeking unquestioning compliance, undervaluing critical thinking, and paying insufficient respect to the moral autonomy of the child. Such criticisms have been refuted (see, for example, Glanzer, 1998, 2003; Lickona, 1996; Kristjánsson, 2013) and we should certainly not interpret the emphasis on "training" or habituation in *The Abolition of Man* as endorsing a crude behaviorism either. Unlike King and Ketley, Lewis is a staunch defender of freedom and explains: "The task of the modern educator is not to cut down jungles but to irrigate deserts. The right defense against false sentiments is to inculcate just sentiments" (1978, p. 14).

Seeing the "task of the modern educator" being to "irrigate deserts" (rather than to "cut down jungles") is not the view of a behaviorist. Nor should we equate inculcation of "just sentiments" (the task of good parents and teachers) with behaviorism. An example will illustrate the difference. Many schools that implement "positive behavior strategies" or "assertive discipline techniques" (Canter and Canter, 2001) are heavily influenced by the behaviorism of Skinner, whose rats were placed in what has become known in psychology as a "Skinner Box." Food was released if they pushed a lever; the "right" behavior was rewarded and the rats came to associate an action with a particular result. Informed by Skinner, the assumption of many school leaders is that students modify their behavior as a result of consequences as they will have formed a "functional relation" between the two. It is often argued that behaviorism "explains the interaction between human behavior and environmental factors" (Maag, 2004, p. 15). This is a far cry from Lewis' ethical understanding that phenomena in the external world "merit" certain responses from human beings who perceive and judge well.

Education, rightly conceived, recognizes that human beings, unlike the rats in Skinner's experiments, have been endowed with the capacity to discern far more than negative or positive associations. If schools or parents or teachers simply seek compliance and behavior modification by rigorously implementing a system of rewards and punishments, they are failing to help young people to develop the range of virtues that enable them to have the right motives for behaving well. Schooling that privileges the cultivation of a range of virtues is in stark contrast to the "behavior management" of schools influenced by the behaviorism of B.F. Skinner, who asserted that "the problem is to induce people not to be good but to behave well" (1971, p. 70).

Today the behavior policies of many schools actually militate against holding students to account, and an important opportunity for moral education is lost, as the focus is often on "inappropriate" (rather than "wrong") *behavior* rather than the *character* of the learner. For instance, a recent guide for school leaders gave the following instructions: "in addressing inappropriate behavior you should always make it clear that it is the behavior and not the person you are critical of" (Hook and Vass, 2011, p. 44). The "Christian" version of this misconception is to focus on the "sin" rather than the "sinner," which can militate against a realistic appraisal about how the person (rather than just the behavior) needs to change. The relation between character education and Christianity has been explored (Pike, 2009b), but in both simply focusing on behavior is not education as it dehumanizes. Significantly, in *Beyond Freedom and Dignity*, Skinner directly attacked the central thesis that Lewis advanced in *The Abolition of Man*:

> C.S. Lewis put it quite bluntly: Man is being abolished . . . Lewis cannot have meant the human species, for not only is it not being abolished, it is filling the earth. We are told that what is being threatened is . . . man as a person not a thing . . . What is being abolished is . . . the inner man . . . the man defended by the literatures of freedom and dignity. His abolition has long been overdue.
>
> Skinner, 1971, p. 200

Skinner asserts the importance of moving away "from the miraculous to the natural" and of going "beyond" such "unscientific" anachronisms in order to make "scientific progress" (like that of the National Institute for Co-ordinated Experiments in *That Hideous Strength* (Lewis, 2005)).

> To man *qua* man we readily say good riddance. Only by dispossessing him can we turn to the real causes of human behavior . . . from the miraculous to the natural . . . Science has probably never demanded a more sweeping change in a traditional way of thinking about a subject; nor has there ever been a more important subject. In the traditional picture a person perceives the world around him, selects features to be perceived . . . judges them good or bad . . . and may be held responsible for his action and justly rewarded or punished for its consequences.
>
> Skinner, 1971, p. 200

Contrary to this, Lewis defended human dignity and our ability to choose well and act upon the world on the basis of our "miraculous" moral sense (or character). Skinner (and others) want to replace this with the "natural" and it is important to clarify the sense in which the word "natural" is used in *The Abolition of Man*. Lewis refers to "Nature," as the opposite of "the Human, the Spiritual, and the Supernatural" (1978, p. 48), as belonging to "the world of quantity, as against the world of quality," and "of that which knows no values," as against that which both has and perceives values so that we reduce something "to the level of 'Nature' in the sense that we suspend our judgement of value about it" (p. 48). The final step is "reducing our own species to the level of mere Nature."

This is illustrated in *Prince Caspian* when the Pevensies are attacked by a great grey bear. Susan fails to shoot the bear with an arrow because she thinks it may be a talking animal rather than a dumb beast. When they have recovered, Lucy tells Susan that a horrible idea has come into her head and she says:

> Wouldn't it be dreadful if some day, in our own world, at home, men started going wild inside, like the animals here, and still looked like men, so that you'd never know which were which?
>
> Lewis, 2009, p. 135

The abolition of character: The "Controllers"

In the third section of *The Abolition of Man*, Lewis describes the "Controllers" or "Conditioners," an Elite or the Establishment that exert control over the population, do away with traditional values, and curtail freedom through schooling. Relatively little appears to have been written on this by Lewis scholars (see Kreeft, 1994; Baggett *et al.*, 2008) but it applies to schooling in the twenty-first century, whether in higher education or at secondary, middle or elementary school level and in both secular and Christian contexts.

Lewis is wary of an "omnicompetent state" (1978, p. 43) and "the power of majorities over minorities" and of "government over the people" (p. 40). Of course, the liberal democratic state already seeks to mold its citizens in its own image through education (Pike, 2007) and to inculcate "faith" in democracy so that we "believe in" this way of life (Pike, 2008). Yet morality is not decided by majority vote and there will, increasingly, be a choice between "religious freedom" and "rendering to Caesar" (Pike, 2009a). Indeed, there are significant differences between "democracy" and the *Tao* (Pike, 2011).

Lewis foresees the "rule of the Conditioners over the conditioned human material, the world of post-humanity" (1978, p. 51) and an "education" where:

> Judgments of value are to be produced in the pupil as part of the conditioning. Whatever *Tao* there is will be the product, not the motive of education. The conditioners have been emancipated from all that … *"Good" and "Bad", applied to them, are words without content*: for it is from them that the content of these words is henceforward to be derived.
>
> Lewis, 1978, p. 45, my italics

Writing in 1943, this abolition of man is what "nearly all men in all nations are at present labouring to produce" (Lewis, 1978, p. 51). In questions that are redolent of those posed by C.S. Lewis, Professor Brenda Almond, the respected British ethicist, has reviewed the ways in which the state increasingly expects people in a diverse, plural society to celebrate and approve of lifestyles and practices that are contrary to their fundamental beliefs and asks:

> Must we approve as well as permit? Must we refrain from judgment? Can we not condemn what we ourselves think is bad? *Or is it wrong even to think in terms of bad and good?* Is moral neutrality the new virtue?
>
> Almond, 2010, p. 132, my italics

In the name of "tolerance" the "Controllers," as Lewis called them, seek to coerce universities, colleges, schools, families, charities, and businesses to approve of and even celebrate beliefs and practices which directly contradict their own if they are to receive state support. This affects private as well as public institutions in higher education where government underwrites student loans. Almond asks how this can have happened "in countries like Britain and the USA in which tolerance and liberty, especially freedom of religion and freedom of thought and of speech, are amongst their highest political ideals?" (2010, p. 139). It also has serious implications for parenting (Pike, 2014), as "this involves claiming for the state a right to replace parental values, which may favor traditional family life, with an approach to children's moral education that is directed by its own experts and ethical advisers and based on quite contrary ethical assumptions" (Almond, 2010, p. 139).

Importantly, "the ground on which these advisers promote tolerance is not that tolerance has value in itself, but simply the belief that no way of life is any more valuable than any other" (Almond, 2010, p. 139). These "experts" sound very much like Lewis' "Controllers" and he reminds us that a time is coming when we will witness "the rejection of the concept of value altogether" (1978, p. 38): "Values are now [regarded as] mere natural phenomena. Judgments of value are to be produced in the pupil as part of the conditioning" (1978, p. 37). Yet clearly:

> ... character cannot develop out of values "nominated" for promotion, "consciously chosen" by a committee, negotiated by a group of diverse

> professionals, or enacted into law by legislators. Such values have, by their very nature, lost the quality of sacredness, their commanding character, and thus their power to inspire and to shame.
>
> Hunter, 2000, p. 225

The Controllers preside over the commodification of virtue itself, as their underlying philosophy will not permit them to describe these virtues *as* virtues but only as "desirable values" or "choices" or "preferences," and these "politically correct" values can change with public opinion, as human beings will believe they are able to determine morality. Schooling should enable students to become discerning readers of the world in which they live (Pike, 2005, 2007, 2013).

In concluding, one might be forgiven for asking, given that the *Tao* presents "universal" virtues from different traditions and cultures, why Lewis thought the Controllers would abandon it. After all, Lewis writes as a "character educator" more than a "Christian educator" in *The Abolition of Man*. Arguably, not only do the Controllers seek to undermine Christian ethics, they have also abandoned common ethics (Natural Law), claiming not to believe any one way of living to be better or worse than another. They are the true descendants of Gaius and Titius.

Yet the Controllers' stated position is inconsistent because they are also closet behaviorists who believe they can influence humanity to move beyond ideas such as human dignity, freedom, and virtue. As "comprehensive" liberals they will claim to defend the "autonomy" of the child, encourage "values clarification," and abhor character education. They will associate virtue theory—and the promotion of virtue—with conservative politics, preferring "social justice" to the obligation to work on "individual" or "personal" virtues. As they recognize that virtue (or an awareness of the lack of it) may lead to faith, the Controllers will set themselves implacably against it; Natural Law may lead to divine law and reason to revelation.

Acknowledgments

I should like to thank Professors Tom Lickona, Perry Glanzer, and Michael Ward for sharing their thoughts about the "Controllers;" Lydia Pike for research; and the John Templeton Foundation for funding the Narnian Virtues project during 2015–2019.

Notes

1 Extracts by C.S. Lewis © copyright C.S. Lewis pte Ltd.
2 Extracts by C.S. Lewis © copyright C.S. Lewis pte Ltd.
3 Extracts by C.S. Lewis © copyright C.S. Lewis pte Ltd.

Works cited

Almond, B. (2010), "Education for tolerance: cultural difference and family values," *Journal of Moral Education*, 39 (2), 131–143.

Aquinas, Thomas (1911 [1948]), *Summa Theologica* (trans. Fathers of the English Dominican Province). Notre Dame, IN: Christian Classics.

Aristotle (1987), *The Nichomachean Ethics* (trans. J.E.C. Weldon). New York: Prometheus Books.

Baggett, D., Habermas, G.R. and Walls, J.L. (eds.) (2008), *C.S. Lewis as Philosopher: Truth, Goodness and Beauty*. Downers Grove, IL: Intervarsity Press.

Berkowitz, M.W. and Bier, M.C. (2004), "Research-based character education," *Annals of the American Academy of Political and Social Science*, 591, 72–85.

Burke, E. (1757 [1958]), *A Philosophical Enquiry into the Origin of Our Idea of the Sublime and Beautiful* (ed. J.T. Boulton). London: Routledge & Kegan Paul.

Canter, L. and Canter, M. (2001), *Assertive Discipline: Positive Behavior Management for Today's Classroom*. Bloomington, IN: Solution Tree.

Cicero (1999), *De Republica* (trans. J. Zetzel). Cambridge: Cambridge University Press

Elshtain, J.B. (2008), "The Abolition of Man. C.S. Lewis' prescience concerning things to come," in D. Baggett, G.R. Habermas and J.L. Walls (eds.), *C.S. Lewis as Philosopher: Truth, Goodness and Beauty*. Downers Grove, IL: Intervarsity Press, pp. 85–95.

Glanzer, P.L. (1998), "The character to seek justice," *Phi Delta Kappan*, 79 (6), 434.

Glanzer, P. (2003), "Did the moral education establishment kill character? An Autopsy of *The Death of Character*," *Journal of Moral Education*, 32 (2003): 291–306.

Higgins, C. (2010), "Work and flourishing: Williams' critique of morality and its implications for professional ethics," *Journal of Philosophy of Education*, 44 (2/3), 211–236.

Hoff-Sommers, C. (1985), "Ethical relativism," in D. Eberly (ed.), *The Content of America's Character: Recovering Civic Virtue*. New York: Madison Books, pp. 163–174.

Hook, P. and Vass, A. (2011), *Behaviour Management Pocketbook*. Alresford: Teachers' Pocketbooks.

Hunter, J.D. (2000), *The Death of Character*. New York: Basic Books.

Kant, I. (1960 [1974]), *Observations on the Feeling of the Beautiful and Sublime* (trans. J.T. Goldthwaite). Berkeley, CA: University of California Press.

King, A. and Ketley, M. (1939), *The Control of Language: A Critical Approach to Reading and Writing*. London: Longmans, Green & Co.

Kohn, A. (1997), "How not to teach values: A critical look at character education," *Phi Delta Kappan*, 78 (6), 429–439.

Kreeft, P. (1994), *C.S. Lewis for the Third Millennium: Six Essays on The Abolition of Man*. San Francisco, CA: Ignatius Press.

Kristjánsson, K. (2013), "Ten myths about character, virtue and virtue education—plus three well-founded misgivings," *British Journal of Education*, 61 (3), 1–19.

Lewis, C.S. (1943 [1978]), *The Abolition of Man—Or Reflections on Education with Special Reference to the Teaching of English in the Upper Forms of Schools*. Glasgow: Fount.

Lewis, C.S. (1945 [2005]), *That Hideous Strength*. London: HarperCollins.

Lewis, C.S. (1952 [1981]), *Mere Christianity*. London: Fount.

Lewis, C. S. (1951 [2009]), *Prince Caspian*. London: Collins.

Lickona, T. (1996), "The decline and fall of American civilization: Can character education reverse the slide?," *Currents in Modern Thought: Educating for Character*, June, pp. 285–307.

Longinus, D. (1964), *On the Sublime* (ed. D.A. Russell). Oxford: Clarendon Press.

Maag, J.W. (2004), *Behavior Management: From Theoretical Implications to Practical Applications* (2nd edn.). London: Wadsworth/Thompson Learning.

McDowell, J. and Hostetler, B. (1994), *Right from Wrong: What You Need to Know to Help Youth Make Right Choices*. Dallas, TX: Word Publishing.

Miller, L. (2008), *The Magician's Book—A Sceptic's Adventures in Narnia*. New York: Back Bay Books.

Pike, M.A. (2005), "Citizenship education and faith schools: What should children in Christian schools understand and appreciate about a liberal and secular society?," *Journal of Education and Christian Belief*, 9 (1), 35–46.

Pike, M.A. (2007), "The state and citizenship education in England: A curriculum for subjects or citizens?," *Journal of Curriculum Studies*, 39 (4), 471–489.
Pike, M.A. (2008), "Faith in citizenship? On teaching children to believe in liberal democracy", *British Journal of Religious Education*, 30 (2), 113–122.
Pike, M.A. (2009a), "Religious freedom and rendering to Caesar: Reading democratic and faith-based values in curriculum, pedagogy and policy," *Oxford Review of Education*, 35 (2), 133–146.
Pike, M.A. (2009b), "Judeo-Christian sources of character education: Learning from England's most academically improved academy," *Journal of Research in Character Education*, 7 (1), 25–40.
Pike, M.A. (2011), "Ethical English teaching: Learning democratic values or living by the Tao?," *Changing English: Studies in Culture and Education*, 18 (4), 351–359.
Pike, M.A. (2012), "'The Trees of Knowledge and Life Growing Together' in the educational vision of C. S. Lewis," *Changing English: Studies in Culture and Education*, 19 (2), 249–259.
Pike, M.A. (2013), *Mere Education: C.S. Lewis as Teacher for Our Time.* Cambridge: Lutterworth Press.
Pike, M.A. (2014), "C.S. Lewis: Christian educator for a post-Christian era," *Sehnsucht: The C.S. Lewis Journal*, 7/8, 63–88.
Pike, M.A. (2015), *Ethical English: Teaching English as Spiritual, Moral and Religious Education*. London: Bloomsbury.
Pike, M.A., Lickona, T. and Nesfield, V. (2015), "Narnian virtues: C.S. Lewis as character educator," *Journal of Character Education*, 11 (2), 71–86.
Skinner, B.F. (1971), *Beyond Freedom and Dignity*. Harmondsworth: Penguin.
Tankard, P. (2007), "Didactic pleasures: Learning in C.S. Lewis' Narnia," *SEVEN: An Anglo-American Literary Review*, 24, 65–86.

4

So How *Should* We Teach English?

Charlie W. Starr
Independent Scholar

Introduction

On the first day of each semester, I walk into the classroom and tell my freshmen that I'm there to "learn 'em some good English." The fact that only half of them giggle tells me that I should either stay away from comedy or I have my work cut out for me. It's typically the latter. We think of Lewis as a great writer of apologetics and fantasy literature, but he was also an English professor—that's what he did for a living. As a fellow purveyor of trades grammatical and literary, I am grateful for the opportunity to present here his thoughts on teaching literature.

The impetus for this discussion is simple enough: in chapter one of *The Abolition of Man*, Lewis reveals what he believes to be the wrong way to teach literature in English classes—to relegate it entirely to the realm of personal, subjective, opinion without any knowledge value. The obvious contrasting question, then, is "so how *should* we teach literature?" Simple enough. But the answer isn't, and we've got to get it right. If we don't, we'll find ourselves caught up in the same ineffective, marginalized cultural position that has been the hallmark of evangelical Christianity for far too long. Captured by Enlightenment (rather than biblical) paradigms of thought,[1] we've failed to understand what literature is for.[2] So if we want to find out how Lewis would have us *teach* (and learn from) literature, we have to know what he thought *about* literature.

The gravity of the problem we're facing was suggested decades ago by Lewis himself in his essay "Horrid Red Things," when he said there are two things Christians must do to defend the faith. The first, easily understood, is that we must defend the supernatural elements of Christianity. The second is that we must teach people the difference between reasoning and imagining (Lewis, 1970, p. 69). I believe this latter point was a message *for believers* as well as non-believers: that we have forgotten the differences between reason and imagination and as such have forgotten what literature, among other arts, is for. The mistake I'm alluding to is a subtle one. It is the belief that the primary purpose of literature is to teach truth. It's not, but I realize that saying so is a shock to some. Clearly, I need to explain what I mean; hopefully I can.

At first, this mistaken view about literature seems easily defended with proof texts from C.S. Lewis himself. For example, in discussing the modern artist's obsession with *originality*, Lewis writes that "in literature and art, no man who bothers about originality will ever be original: whereas if you simply try to tell the truth (without caring twopence how often it has been told before) you will, nine times out of ten, become original without ever having noticed it" (1952, p. 191). The secondary point of this quote seems pretty clear: when writing literature, try to "tell the truth." But such a reading of Lewis is quickly complicated when we encounter what he wrote specifically about the *purposes* of literature: "I have rejected the views that literature is to be valued (*a*) for telling us truths about life, [or] (*b*) as an aid to culture" (1961, p. 130). Perhaps context explains the seeming contradiction between these passages, or perhaps Lewis' ideas about the purpose of literature evolved.[3]

But here, then, is the problem we're given to solve by the opening chapter of *The Abolition of Man*:

1. To argue the existence of objective values, Lewis uses examples of how literature should *not* be taught or thought about.
2. If we then ask how Lewis *would* have us teach literature, we could begin with the answer, "In the opposite manner from what he derides in *Abolition*." This will prove a solid start, but we'll quickly discover that Lewis doesn't think it answer enough.
3. Therefore, to avoid a critical mistake regarding how literature can be used to teach, we will have to look elsewhere in the Lewis corpus with an eye toward understanding Lewis' ideas about the very nature and purpose of literature. Are we meant to use it to learn or teach truth? If not, how can we use it to teach at all?

If Christians ever wish to be culturally relevant again, if we ever wish to teach and make literature, movies, and music which impact the culture in which we find ourselves, if we ever want to do more than make stories and movies for our own niche markets, we have to understand what literature is for. And we can do that by answering the question, how would C.S. Lewis have us teach literature? Let's begin to find the answers with *The Abolition of Man*.

The argument in *Abolition*

What I most admire about Lewis' writing style is that he never takes the approach to a problem we'd expect anyone to take. Here, in *Abolition*, Lewis has every intention of discussing a major philosophical issue: the existence of objective values. How will he approach such an erudite topic? By beginning with grade school textbooks.

In chapter one of *Abolition*, Lewis takes issue with certain passages he finds in the pseudonymous *Green Book*, "a little book on English" intended for pre-college education (Lewis, 1947, p. 13). At first, Lewis doesn't seem to take issue with the book's instruction on English (that is, on literature) at all. His focus is on language and philosophy, and what he objects to are the presuppositions that "all sentences containing a predicate of value" merely express the speaker's emotional state, and, thus, that such statements "don't really matter" (p. 15). Lewis rejects these presuppositions. He rejects the idea that value statements are merely about a person's emotional state and further rejects any notion that emotions are "contrary to reason" (p. 19). I would also suggest that implicit in Lewis' thinking here is a position about the nature of literature as a device for evoking emotion.

A false dichotomy to which we can easily fall is that philosophy exists to appeal to the thinking self and literature exists to appeal to our feelings. A phrase in *Abolition* provides an inkling of this idea. For Lewis, the problem is not merely that emotions are shut down if we teach their irrelevance. It's also that this teaching removes from young students the "possibility of having certain experiences which thinkers of more authority" have long considered worthwhile (1947, p. 20). Lewis refers to this removal in surgical terms as a cutting out which is being replicated elsewhere in education under "the same general anaesthetic" (p. 20). For Lewis, literature, and the kind of language associated with it, do not exist to evoke emotion but to highlight certain qualities of the objects brought to a reader's attention, qualities which may then evoke emotional responses. The distinction is subtle, but it will prove important, as we'll see later.

While Lewis' initial focus in *Abolition* is on language and philosophy, it is not long before he turns to the implications of the ideas expressed by *The Green Book*'s authors (whom he calls Gaius and Titius; 1947, p. 13) on how we perceive and teach literature. In the examples Lewis then offers as mistaken approaches, he objects to any method of teaching English that does so by debunking literary (or poetic) language.

The first example is from chapter four of *The Green Book*. In it, the authors offer an advertisement for a cruise that is intended to show their young readers how to avoid sales propaganda. This advertisement, Lewis summarizes, "tells us that those who buy tickets for this cruise will go 'across the Western Ocean where Drake and Devon sailed'" (1947, p. 17). Lewis agrees that it's a bad piece of writing intended to exploit the feelings people experience when they visit historical places. But Gaius and Titius miss an opportunity to teach what their book is supposed to teach: English. All they do is point out that the language of the advertisement is a lie. Anyone who visits historical places will not have the same adventures as Drake and others had. But if this is all the textbook does, the result on the pupil will be that he doesn't think the emotions evoked by a visit to any historical place will be worth having. As Lewis puts it, the student will only learn "that all emotions aroused by local association are themselves contrary to reason and contemptible" (p. 19). In trying to inoculate the student against the dangers of propaganda, *The Green Book* rather shows them that *all* emotional appeals are suspect. What the book should have done, if it were truly intended to teach the "art of English composition" (p. 17), is place the advertisement side by side with a passage from a great writer who makes the same appeal about a historical place with beautiful prose. "They might have used Johnson's famous passage from the *Western Islands*" or "that place in *The Prelude* where Wordsworth describes how the antiquity of London first descended on his mind with 'Weight and power, Power growing under weight'" (p. 18). Placing these pieces of good writing next to the hackneyed writing of the cruise advertisement and pointing out how the former is superior to the latter would not destroy the idea that there are such things as proper emotional sentiments, and, furthermore, it would actually teach "a lesson in literature" (p. 18).

The second example Lewis offers regards the rejection of poetic language that is specifically anthropomorphic. He takes his example from a different book, one authored by someone he refers to as Orbilius. This writer "chooses for 'debunking' a silly bit of writing on horses, where these animals are praised as the 'willing servants' of the early colonists in Australia" (1947, pp. 20–21). Now he does compare the writing to a better piece of writing about animals, but his only defining factor for saying the one is superior to the other is that it is factually more accurate (p. 21, note 7). The result for young pupils of claiming that it is illogical or untruthful to read any human qualities into animals is subtle but clear: "Some pleasure in their own ponies and dogs they will have lost; some incentive to cruelty or neglect they will have received: some pleasure in their own knowingness will have entered their minds" (p. 22).

Now why is it that these teachers of English aren't teaching English? In fact, they seem to be doing the opposite—they seem to be teaching that the imaginative language of literature is insignificant. Lewis suggests they might be teaching this way as a philosophical choice but then thinks other reasons more likely: (1) that it's simply too hard to explain *why* bad treatment of emotional content is, indeed, bad and that it's instead much easier to debunk the emotions themselves; (2) that because of the age in which they find themselves, these authors are more concerned about protecting children from propaganda. But the defense pupils need against false sentiments (the kinds of sentiments evoked by propaganda) is not to be told all sentiment is bunk. Rather, the "right defence against false sentiments is to inculcate just sentiments" (1947, p. 24). Even these, though, may not be the truest reasons for this wrong approach to teaching English. Lewis fears the real reason literature is being approached in such non-literary ways is that these authors simply don't believe in "the doctrine of objective value, the belief that certain attitudes are really true, and others really false, to the kind of thing the universe is and the kind of things we are" (p. 29). If there are no objective "just sentiments" (p. 26), then all sentiments—that is, all emotional reactions—are suspect with no sure connection to either factual or moral truth. This is what Lewis objects to: the teaching of literature in a way that rejects the objective values to which aesthetically excellent texts (good literature as opposed to bad writing) point. Lewis would argue that emotional states can indeed be "in harmony with reason" or "out of harmony with reason" (p. 29), but, if we don't train up our students in the appropriate emotional states before they're even able to reason, they won't be able to tell which sentiments operate in harmony with reason and which merely lie.

The opposite approach

As chapter one of *The Abolition of Man* steers steadily toward the book's primary thesis—the existence of objective values—we may ourselves veer off to continue our discussion on how Lewis would have us teach English. *Abolition* offers the beginnings of a system of literary education. In pointing out the wrong way to teach, Lewis gives us clues about the right way to do it, and, although there is a danger in taking *Abolition* alone as our source for English pedagogy, we should first emphasize the book's positive lessons.

The methods for teaching English that we can glean from *Abolition* are these:

1. *Teach the legitimacy of metaphorical or poetic language.* This is to say that we should see the epistemological value of literature. As Lewis notes in "The Language of Religion,"

> Now it seems to me a mistake to think that our experiences in general can be communicated by precise and literal language . . . The truth seems to me the opposite . . . The very essence of our life as conscious beings, all day and every day, consists of something which cannot be communicated except by hints, similes, metaphors, and the use of those emotions (themselves not very important) which are pointers to it.
>
> 1967, pp. 138, 140

There is much we know which we cannot put into words, or, when we do put it into words, we can only do so through the use of poetic language. As such, poetic language has epistemological value—it can communicate knowledge. At the same time, we'll see, Lewis would *not* have us teaching our youngest students *about* the epistemological value of literature. He would, instead, simply have us take literature seriously—have us teach it as if the poetic (symbolic, metaphorical, anthropomorphical, hyperbolic) language in the text were really saying something about reality.

2. *Help students recognize the difference between good literature and bad writing by offering side-by-side comparisons of the two.* On a slightly larger scale, Lewis frequently talks about the *kinds* of literature that he found beneficial or harmful. Thus he attacks Modern poetry in a poem of his own, "Spartan Nactus," by noting that, after decades of trying, he still could not figure out how an evening could ever suggest to him the image of a patient etherized upon a table ("Spartan," 2015, p. 388, lines 1–6), a satirical hit on the opening of Eliot's "The Love Song of J. Alfred Prufrock." Additionally, in *The Voyage of the Dawn Treader*, Lewis suggests that books of facts and figures for children are inferior in the scene where Eustace enters a dragon's lair: "Most of us know what we should expect to find in a dragon's lair, but, as I said before, Eustace had read only the wrong books. They had a lot to say about exports and imports and governments and drains, but they were weak on dragons" ("Voyage," 1980, p. 92).[4] On the level of comparing individual texts (as Lewis suggests in *Abolition*), we find a few examples in his literary criticism. In "Variation in Shakespeare and Others," for example, Lewis opens with a close comparison of texts from Milton and Shakespeare, each treating the same subject but Milton via a method Lewis labels "*construction*" and Shakespeare through a technique of "*variation*" ("Variation," 1969a, p. 76).[5] As the essay progresses, Lewis focuses on variation, offering texts that both succeed and fail[6] in the use of the technique, with particular cuts against Shirley's application of the method in drama (pp. 84–87).

3. *Do not guard against false sentiments (the kind evoked by propaganda, for example) by debunking all sentiment. Instead, expose students to literature that fills them with just sentiments.* As Lewis puts it so metaphorically well, "The task of the modern educator is not to cut down jungles but to irrigate deserts" (*Abolition*, 1947, p. 24). And Lewis would have us do this for our students from an early age, even before they are capable of reason.[7]

4. *Inculcate just sentiments.* We have to be careful about this final lesson. It is the most important, but the most easily misunderstood. It calls us to a critical

truth in *Abolition*, but demands that we look beyond this book if we want to avoid a significant mistake. To begin, though, Lewis is arguing that we should teach our young how they ought to feel about certain things:

> Aristotle says that the aim of education is to make the pupil like and dislike what he ought. When the age for reflective thought comes, the pupil who has been thus trained in "ordinate affections" or "just sentiments" will easily find the first principles in Ethics: but to the corrupt man they will never be visible at all and he can make no progress in that science. Plato before him had said the same. The little human animal will not at first have the right responses. It must be trained to feel pleasure, liking, disgust, and hatred at those things which really are pleasant, likeable, disgusting, and hateful . . . "All this before he is of an age to reason; so that when Reason at length comes to him, then, bred as he has been, he will hold out his hands in welcome and recognize her because of the affinity he bears to her."
>
> 1947, p. 27

This passage may be the thematic climax of *Abolition*'s first chapter. Using English education as his access point, Lewis has been working his way here from the beginning, and the rest of the book will take up the issue of objective truth and goodness to its completion. Why, then, do I say there's a danger to avoid in teaching just sentiments?

The problem with *using* literature

A failure in teaching children how to feel about various aspects of reality will occur when teachers mistakenly think they should spend their time *telling* students what they *ought* to feel. In addition to being a terrible way to teach literature, this approach to inculcating just sentiments (right feelings) will fail. If we tell students how they ought to feel, they will stop wanting to feel that way. Lewis makes this abundantly clear in "Sometimes Fairy Stories May Say Best What's To Be Said." There he notes that some people seemed to think his method of creating the Narnia stories involved wanting to say something to children about Christianity, choosing the fairy tale as his method of doing so, making a list of Christian truths he wanted to tell, and creating allegories to tell those truths. Says Lewis, "This is all pure moonshine" ("Sometimes," 1966,

p. 36). His purpose was not didactic, but at the same time he *did* recognize a goal for his stories regarding the sentiments people have toward religion:

> I thought I saw how stories of this kind could steal past a certain inhibition which had paralysed much of my own religion in childhood. Why did one find it so hard to feel as one was told one ought to feel about God or about the sufferings of Christ? I thought the chief reason was that one was told one ought to. An obligation to feel can freeze feelings … But supposing that by casting all these things into an imaginary world, stripping them of their stained-glass and Sunday school associations, one could make them for the first time appear in their real potency? Could one not thus steal past those watchful dragons?
>
> p. 37

The danger we face in trying to use literature to teach kids *how* to feel rightly about all they experience in life will be to fall into the trap of trying to tell them what they *ought* to be feeling. They can't be *told*. They have to be *shown*—and this probably without telling them why we're doing it (at least at first). Lewis makes a sharp distinction between art and teaching, between culture and pedantry. Thus, in "Christianity and Culture," when he speaks of Christians being involved in cultural activities such as writing stories in order to resist the abuses of culture, he does "not mean that a Christian should take money for supplying one thing (culture) and use the opportunity thus gained to supply a quite different thing (homiletics and apologetics). That is stealing" (2000a, p. 79).

The problem with trying to draw lessons on how to teach English from *The Abolition of Man*, alone, is that we may end up approaching the contents and thought modes of literature in the same way we approach those of philosophy (as Lewis does in *Abolition*). C.S. Lewis is not to blame for this mistake. Our failure to look completely at what Lewis said about literature would be. The qualities of partitioning, abstract analysis, and propositional truth finding that we practice in philosophy and theology have their place in English studies in the form of literary criticism. But literature involves more than abstract analysis. There is a foundational component to literature, one that is both imaginative and experiential. Recall that Lewis says right feeling is a thing to be taught even before students are capable of reasoning. This foundational element calls for a different approach to the teaching of literature. Lewis would not want us to tell our students how they ought to feel. That will "freeze feeling." Instead, he would want us to put our students through experiences of the best literature—experiences that will teach right feeling by *evoking* it. In other words, rather than telling students what they ought to feel, literature (or any good art) can make them feel it. Experiences create emotional responses. These responses may be in harmony with reason or out of harmony with it, but we don't want to read stories with our students only to tell them, "And this is the lesson to be learned," or "This is what you ought to feel about that." If we tried that method to instill just sentiments in our students, we would fail.

Literary uses and misuses

To understand more fully how Lewis would have us teach literature, then, we have to know what he thought the purpose of literature was. Let's begin even more basically with what Lewis thought about *literary language*. I want to return now to a distinction we briefly considered at the beginning of this essay: that poetic language doesn't exist to evoke emotion but certain qualitative experiences. Lewis explicates this idea in his essay, "The Language of Religion." There he says that literary or "poetic" language "does not consist either in discharging or arousing more emotion" than "scientific" or "ordinary" language ("Language," 1967, p. 130). While literary language may sometimes do this, "it does not follow that the expression of emotion is always its sole, or even chief function" (p. 132). On the contrary, "Poetic language often expresses emotion not for its own sake but in order to inform us about the object which aroused the emotion" (p. 132). The emphasis of poetic language is not on emotion but on an object of experience.

If I use plain language to say "it's cold out," you understand my meaning easily enough, but all I've expressed is a quantity, a state (this is even more so the case if I use scientific language: "it's ten degrees below zero outside"). If I say, however, that "it's as cold out there as a Chihuahua on the South Pole," you will receive from me not only a statement about the *fact* that it's cold but something of my personal response to the *experience* of that cold. The simile I've used does not call you to an emotional response (not initially) but to a sensory one. Granted my poetic language isn't very good, but in it I'm asking you to picture Antarctic regions combined with the presence of the most easily chilled canine species on the planet. If you happen to own a Chihuahua, you might recall moments when your little dog was all a tremble. *And it is these images, then, that may evoke an emotional response from you.* Lewis argues that poetic language "is by no means merely an expression, nor a stimulant, of emotion, but a real medium of information" (1967, p. 134). And even though poetic language may "stimulate emotion, by expressing emotion," it does so "in order to show us the object to which such emotion would be the response" (p. 134).

The significance of this distinction is epistemological in nature. Since poetic language treats not merely of human emotion but of experiences of concrete reality, it is clearly valuable for its ability to allow the reader to encounter truth. That a thing is "imaginary" becomes an epistemologically derogatory term when we refuse to see the connection between the imagination and the real, that is, between the imagination's ability to create encounters with the real through poetic language and through story. An imaginary thing may yet be true. And a fiction may yet show us reality. This idea of the epistemological significance of imagination is vital to understanding Lewis' thoughts about literature, so we must explore it further.

From "Horrid Red Things," the essay referenced in the Introduction, I hinted at our contemporary failure to understand the difference between imagination and reason. To this we should add a contemporary failure to understand what the imagination *even is*. We have especially been taught that imagination has little practical purpose and little connection to knowing anything. That which is in the imagination is unreal. That which is unreal has no truth value, yes? I answer, "No," but let's back up a moment.

Lewis famously defines imagination as the "organ of meaning," while reason is the "organ of truth" ("Bluspels and Flalansferes," 1939a, p. 157). Lewis emphasizes that without imagination, knowing either truth or falsehood is impossible. To say "the sky is blue" is something we will only recognize as a truth statement if we know the meanings of the words in the statement (and imagination as the organ of meaning makes this possible). At the same time, we can have false images mixed with true ideas. The example in "Horrid Red Things" is of a little girl who knows what poison is but thinks it's always red (1970, p. 70). Additionally, there may be meanings in our imaginations that do not lead us to truth statements but to apprehensions we cannot put into words (though words may hint at such things as we saw in "The Language of Religion"). Have you ever "fallen in love" with a song the first time you heard it? And when friends asked why you enjoyed the song so much, were you then dumbfounded by any attempt at explanation? Clearly, such songs have meaning to us, even if we can't articulate them. And this is a key point: what happens in the imagination may lead to understandings we cannot fully explain—to knowledge which we are certain smacks of encounters with reality (and then truth), but which we may never (or at least not immediately) be able to verbalize.

I apply it to literature this way: in the reading of a story, I am taken on an imaginative experience. While in that experience I may occasionally stop to ponder its significance, but for the most part I am caught up in a concrete world (concrete even if fictional because it's made so by my imagination's ability to copy sensory experience). In that world I encounter multivalent meanings, some conscious, some semi-conscious, some describable, some only vaguely intuited. If the author whose book I'm reading has done his job, my experience of the work will cause me to respond emotionally to it. If he has taken me through an experience which tells something of the true nature of *my own* world, and if I am drawn by the aesthetic pleasure of my encounter, then he has inspired in me not just a sentiment—a subjective emotional response—but a just sentiment, an emotional response that corresponds with the way things really are (and thus we return to *Abolition*).

Lewis makes this point in defending Milton. In his *A Preface to Paradise Lost*, Lewis takes up a critique against Milton rendered by Dr. I.A. Richards who attacked *Paradise Lost* for being full of "stock responses," or "deliberately organized attitude[s]" that get in the way of the literary experience (Lewis, *Preface*, 1942, p. 55). These stock responses are the very same "just sentiments" Lewis argued we should be inculcating in our students in *The Abolition of Man*. Where Richards sees them as propaganda for a particular view of the world (p. 52), Lewis sees them as utterly necessary for virtue: "Every virtue is a *habitus*—i.e. a *good* stock response" (2000a, p. 82). And what is needed for virtue to endure is precisely this. "Moral theologians, I believe, tell us to fly at sight from temptations to faith or chastity. If that is not (in Dr Richards's words) a "stock", "stereotyped", "conventional" response, I do not know what is" (p. 82).

But where Richards argues that such stock responses are propaganda or cheap rhetoric, Lewis retorts that, while rhetoric purports to move our minds toward some "practical resolve" (by inculcating just sentiments to do so[8]), "poetry aims at producing something more like vision than it is like action" (*Preface*, 1942, p. 53). And this is key to understanding *how* literature inculcates just sentiments through the experiential imagination:

> Certain things, if not seen as lovely or detestable, are not being correctly seen at all ... Hence the awakening and moulding of the reader's or hearer's emotions is a necessary element in that vision of concrete reality which poetry hopes to produce. Very roughly, we might almost say that in Rhetoric imagination is present for the sake of passion (and, therefore, in the long run, for the sake of action), while in poetry passion is present for the sake of imagination, and therefore, in the long run, for the sake of wisdom or spiritual health—the rightness and richness of a man's total response to the world. Such rightness, of course, has a tendency to contribute indirectly to right action, besides being in itself exhilarating and tranquillizing; that is why the old critics were right enough when they said that Poetry taught by delighting, or delighted by teaching.
>
> 1942, pp. 53–54

In other words, literature is capable of creating a concrete vision of reality in the imagination, one that will produce a by-product result: wisdom and perhaps spiritual health. But poetic literature cannot teach by telling people what to think. It can only do so when its primary purposes, achieved in the imagination, are to *exhilarate*, or to make *tranquil*—that is, to *delight*.

Having looked at the epistemological implications of imagination and literary language, we can now consider literature itself. Lewis definitely sees a connection between art and knowledge. In *The Great Divorce*, for example, a painter who has just come into heaven is told that "When you painted on earth . . . it was because you caught glimpses of Heaven in the earthly landscape. The success of your painting was that it enabled others to see the glimpses too" (1973, p. 83). And such glimpses, as Lewis himself found in "inanimate nature and marvelous literature" (notice that these glimpses are either direct or imaginative experiences) evoke in us an experience of "intense longing" (*The Pilgrim's Regress*, 1943, p. 202), an "unsatisfied desire which is itself more desirable than any other satisfaction" (*Surprised by Joy*, 1955, pp. 17–18). Lewis calls this desire "Joy" (p. 18), and Joy is a marker—a stab of desire whose object is not to be found on earth:

> Creatures are not born with desires unless satisfaction for those desires exists. A baby feels hunger: well, there is such a thing as food. A duckling wants to swim: well, there is such a thing as water. Men feel sexual desire: well, there is such a thing as sex. If I find in myself a desire which no experience in this world can satisfy, the most probable explanation is that I was made for another world.
>
> Lewis, *Mere*, 1952, p. 115

Lewis sees the intense desire he calls Joy as an "ontological proof" for the existence of heaven and God (*Regress*, 1943, p. 205). And the implication for literature as a means of arousing Joy in us (through an imaginative experience of aesthetic delight) is that it may potentially point us to the truth of God's existence. It did for C.S. Lewis.

In paradoxical contrast, though, Lewis rejects the idea that the purpose of literature is for the communication or pursuit of truth, transcendent, moral or otherwise. Lewis claims that whatever edification we get from works of fiction or poetry isn't about finding truth in them: "To value them chiefly for reflections which they may suggest to us or morals we may draw from them, is a flagrant instance of 'using' [texts for our own purposes] instead of 'receiving'" [them for what they are] (*Experiment*, 1961, pp. 82–83).[9] Instead, great literature is about a particular activity of imagination; it is about finding new ways of *seeing*—about seeing through the eyes of others:

> The nearest I have yet got to an answer [to the question of literature's value] is that we seek an enlargement of our being. We want to be more than ourselves. Each of us by nature sees the whole world from one point of view with a perspective and a selectiveness peculiar to himself . . . We want to see with other eyes, to imagine with other imaginations, to feel with other hearts, as well as with our own . . . My own eyes are not enough for me, I will see through those of others. Reality, even seen through the eyes of many, is not enough. I will see what others have invented . . . [I]n reading great literature I become a thousand men and yet remain myself . . . Here, as in worship, in love, in moral action, and in knowing, I transcend Myself; and am never more myself than when I do.
>
> 1961, pp. 137, 140–141

In short, Lewis very specifically rejects any view that "literature is to be valued . . . for telling us truths about life" (p. 130). But if so what *is* its purpose? The answer he has just given: a particular kind of experience—an "enlargement of our being."

And a second answer to the purpose of literature is suggested when Lewis says,

> It is a serious matter to choose wholesome recreations: but they would no longer be recreations if we pursued them seriously . . . For a great deal (not all) of our literature was made to be read lightly for entertainment. If we do not read it, in a sense, "for fun" . . . we are not using it as it was meant to be used, and all our criticism of it will be pure illusion. For you cannot judge any artefact except by using it as it was intended. It is no good judging a butter-knife by seeing whether it will saw logs.
>
> 2000a, p. 90

All of this seems to suggest, contrary to what we saw in Part Two of this chapter, that literature has no place in education. It should not be "used" for anything (least of all for revealing moral truth) except certain kinds of experiences and entertainment.

Still we cannot ignore what we've already seen: Lewis values the teaching of English, and he defends poetry as a means of teaching stock responses—true virtues—through delight. I do not think he is being contradictory in his thought. I think the issue for Lewis is one of *emphasis* or *priority*. Though he primarily values literature apart from its truth-bearing potentials, he nevertheless strikes a balance for us between our desires to enjoy literature for what it is on the one hand and use it for education on the other:

> The purpose of education has been described by Milton as that of fitting a man "to perform justly, skillfully, and magnanimously all the offices both private and public, of peace and war." . . . Aristotle would substantially agree with this, but would add the conception that it should also be a preparation for leisure . . . Vocational training, on the other hand, prepares the pupil not for leisure, but for work; it aims at making not a good man but a good banker, a good electrician, a good scavenger, or a good surgeon. You see at once that education is essentially for freemen and vocational training for slaves . . . If education is beaten by training, civilization dies.
>
> "Our English Syllabus," 1939b, pp. 81–82

Here, Lewis clearly accepts the idea that education in literature and the arts has a purpose: preparing the pupil to practice leisure. Doing so will help preserve civilization. The paradoxical twist, perhaps, is to see that the purpose of literature is to entertain us, and great literature, if it entertains well, will also educate without falling into the trap of being merely *educational*.

And so we come round to conclude that teaching poetic texts has a practical purpose, even if that purpose is secondary (or tertiary) to the primary purposes of fiction and poetry—literature can help develop right sentiments in our young. But it can only do this by being what it is, through literary methods—methods that are indirect, imaginative, experiential. I've taken us down a long road to clarify this point. As soon as we try to *use* literature to teach morals, we are in danger of failure. We cannot teach just sentiments to our students by having them read stories and then draw abstract moral statements out of them. Literature can only teach by being what it is—it must be allowed to teach just sentiments by putting readers through experiences, by making them see through the eyes of others, by offering them an imaginative enlargement of their being, and by entertaining and delighting them. This is not to say we cannot analyze literary texts. To do so is the purview of criticism. But the action of inculcating just sentiments occurs through experience in the imagination, while analyzing the meanings of a text is an act of abstract reason. If we do not teach literature in a way that is, in short, *literary*, we will fail to inculcate just sentiments in our pupils because, to paraphrase Lewis, we will be using butter knives to cut logs.

Conclusion

I have to acknowledge that there is a certain sense in which this exploration has failed. If its purpose was to say, "Here is how we should be teaching English" and outline several pedagogical steps toward that end, it has, I grant, offered only a few such suggestions. We've spent most of our time together working through a philosophical foundation from which we might, if time and chapter lengths allowed, develop a set of strategies for teaching *literary* to our pupils, especially in ways that would inculcate just sentiments. Lay the critical foundation and the practical applications will follow. That's my hope. But if I've spent more time exploring how we should *not* teach literature rather than how we should, I am in good company. C.S. Lewis did the same thing in *The Abolition of Man*.[10]

Notes

1 As thoroughly delineated by Malcolm Guite in the pages of his excellent book, *Faith, Hope and Poetry* (2012).

2 I've written about this issue before, including in "Aesthetics vs. Anesthesia" (Starr, 2013).

3 The former quote from *Mere Christianity* appeared in that book in 1952 (though its origins are even earlier); the latter quote in *An Experiment in Criticism* in 1961—but if Lewis' thinking did evolve, then it suggests the perfunctory conclusion that Lewis would not have had us teach literature for any purpose at all. If so, how we teach it wouldn't matter! But given that Lewis taught literature for a living, we cannot draw such a quick and simple conclusion.

4 In fact, Lewis references the importance of reading the right books seven times in *Dawn Treader* (see Devin Brown's *Inside the Voyage of the Dawn Treader*, 2010, pp. 103–104).

5 My thanks to Michael Ward for pointing me toward this and other examples.

6 Even in Shakespeare—p. 83.

7 See *Abolition*, p. 27.

8 Cheap rhetoric, or propaganda, in contrast, would attempt to move our minds via false sentiments.

9 See, especially, all of chapter eight for Lewis' discussion on the connections and disconnections between art and reality and art and truth.

10 Lewis certainly has more to offer us on the teaching of English. To that end Michael Ward suggested to me as additional research such Lewis resources as, "The Idea of an English School" (1939c), "Our English Syllabus" (1939b), "Democratic Education" (2000b), "High and Low Brows" (1969b), "Is English Doomed?" (2000c), "The Parthenon and the Optative" (2000d), and "Lilies That Fester" (2000e). To these I would add, "Sometimes Fairy Stories May Say Best What's To Be Said" (1966), "On Three Ways of Writing for Children" (2000f), "On Stories" (2000g), "Christianity and Culture" (2000a), and *An Experiment in Criticism* (1961).

Works cited

Brown, D. (2010), *Inside the Voyage of the Dawn Treader: A Guide to Exploring the Journey Beyond Narnia*. Grand Rapids, MI: Baker.

Guite, M. (2012), *Faith, Hope and Poetry: Theology and the Poetic Imagination*. Aldershot: Ashgate.

Lewis, C.S. (1939a), "Bluspels and Flalansferes: A Semantic Nightmare," in *Rehabilitations and Other Essays*. Oxford: Oxford University Press, pp. 133–158.

Lewis, C.S. (1939b), "Our English Syllabus," in *Rehabilitations and Other Essays*. Oxford: Oxford University Press, pp. 79–93.

Lewis, C.S. (1939c), "The Idea of an English School," in *Rehabilitations and Other Essays*. Oxford: Oxford University Press, pp. 57–77.

Lewis, C.S. (1942), *A Preface to Paradise Lost*. Oxford: Oxford University Press.

Lewis, C.S. (1943), *The Pilgrim's Regress: An Allegorical Apology for Christianity Reason and Romanticism*. Grand Rapids, MI: Eerdmans.

Lewis, C.S. (1947), *The Abolition of Man—Or Reflections on Education with Special Reference to the Teaching of English in the Upper Forms of Schools*. New York: Macmillan.

Lewis, C.S. (1952), *Mere Christianity* (Christian Library Edition). Westwood, NJ: Barbour.

Lewis, C.S. (1955), *Surprised by Joy: The Shape of My Early Life*. New York: Harcourt Brace Jovanovich.

Lewis, C.S. (1961), *An Experiment in Criticism*. Cambridge: Cambridge University Press.

Lewis, C.S. (1966), "Sometimes Fairy Stories May Say Best What's To Be Said," in *Of Other Worlds: Essays & Stories* (ed. W. Hooper). New York: Harvest, pp. 35–38.

Lewis, C.S. (1967), "The Language of Religion," in *Christian Reflections* (ed. W. Hooper). Grand Rapids, MI: Eerdmans, pp. 129–141.

Lewis, C.S. (1969a), "Variation in Shakespeare and Others," in *Selected Literary Essays* (ed. W. Hooper). Cambridge: Cambridge University Press, pp. 74–87.

Lewis, C.S. (1969b), "High and Low Brows," in *Selected Literary Essays* (ed. W. Hooper). Cambridge: Cambridge University Press, pp. 266–279.

Lewis, C.S. (1970), "Horrid Red Things," in *God in the Dock: Essays on Theology and Ethics* (ed. W. Hooper). Grand Rapids, MI: Eerdmans, pp. 68–71.

Lewis, C.S. (1973), *The Great Divorce: A Dream*. San Francisco, CA: HarperCollins.

Lewis, C.S. (1980), *The Voyage of the Dawn Treader*. New York: HarperCollins.

Lewis, C.S. (2000a), "Christianity and Culture," in *Essay Collection and Other Short Pieces* (ed. L. Walmsley). London: HarperCollins, pp. 71–92.

Lewis, C.S. (2000b), "Democratic Education," in *Essay Collection and Other Short Pieces* (ed. L. Walmsley). London: HarperCollins, pp. 597–600.
Lewis, C.S. (2000c), "Is English Doomed?," in *Essay Collection and Other Short Pieces* (ed. L. Walmsley). London: HarperCollins, pp. 434–437.
Lewis, C.S. (2000d), "The Parthenon and the Optative," in *Essay Collection and Other Short Pieces* (ed. L. Walmsley). London: HarperCollins, pp. 444–446.
Lewis, C.S. (2000e), "Lilies That Fester," in *Essay Collection and Other Short Pieces* (ed. L. Walmsley). London: HarperCollins, pp. 367–377.
Lewis, C.S. (2000f), "On Three Ways of Writing for Children," in *Essay Collection and Other Short Pieces* (ed. L. Walmsley). London: HarperCollins, pp. 505–514.
Lewis, C.S. (2000g), "On Stories," in *Essay Collection and Other Short Pieces* (ed. L. Walmsley). London: HarperCollins, pp. 491–504.
Lewis, C.S. (2015), "Spartan Nactus," in *The Collected Poems of C.S. Lewis: A Critical Edition* (ed. D.W. King). Kent, OH: Kent State University Press, p. 388.
Starr, C.W. (2013), "Aesthetics vs. Anesthesia: C.S. Lewis on the Purpose of Art," in *C.S. Lewis and the Arts: Creativity in the Shadowlands*. Baltimore, MD: Square Halo Books, pp. 115–131.

5

Is *The Abolition of Man* Conservative?

Francis J. Beckwith
Baylor University

Conservative thinkers often cite the *The Abolition of Man* as if it were an essential text in the modern conservative canon. University of Texas philosopher Robert C. Koons includes it in his "short list of conservative classics" (2000, p. 8). Conservative historian Steven F. Hayward (2015) writes, "I can point to one book that, at an early moment, deepened my philosophical conservatism: C.S. Lewis' *The Abolition of Man.*" In his 1956 *New York Times* debate with liberal historian Arthur Schlesinger, Jr., the conservative thinker Russell Kirk opined that "the modern 'liberal' world, as I have come to understand it, is making its way strait toward what C.S. Lewis calls 'the abolition of man'—toward a society devoid of reverence, variety and the higher imagination, in which 'everyone belongs to everyone else,' in which there is collectivism without community, equality without love" (Kirk and Schlesinger, 1956). Political philosopher Peter Lawler, appointed in 2004 by President George W. Bush to the President's Council on Bioethics, wrote in 2000 that "the aim of conservatives for some time now has been to resist what C.S. Lewis called 'the abolition of man.'" The magazine *National Review*, founded by conservative public intellectual William F. Buckley, Jr., lists *The Abolition of Man* as #7 in its 100 best non-fiction books of the twentieth century (*National Review*, 2005).

Because I could produce many more quotes and citations of a similar nature, it may seem obvious that the answer to this chapter's question—"Is *The Abolition of Man* Conservative?"—is an emphatic "yes." However, I want to argue that the "yes" only applies to a certain species of the genus conservatism. There are certain conservatisms with which Lewis' reasoning would not be at home.

Lewis begins *The Abolition of Man* by discussing *The Green Book* and its authors Gaius and Titius, all pseudonyms employed by Lewis, because he did "not want to pillory two modest practicing schoolmasters who were doing the best they knew" (Lewis, 1947, p. 1). *The Green Book* addresses a comment made by Samuel Coleridge about descriptions of a waterfall that Coleridge had heard uttered by two tourists. One tourist said the waterfall was "sublime," while the other said it was "pretty." Although, as Lewis notes, "Coleridge mentally endorsed the first judgment and rejected the second" (p. 2), he was concerned with how the authors of *The Green Book* explained the waterfall's sublimity to their young English readers. They write: "When the man said *That is sublime*, he appeared to be making a remark about the waterfall . . . Actually . . . he was not making a remark about the waterfall, but a remark about his own feelings. What he was saying was really *I have feelings associated in my mind with the word 'Sublime,'* or shortly, *I have sublime feelings*" (p. 2).

As Lewis points out, there is a fundamental difference between attributing a predicate of value to the thing itself—e.g., "The Pietá *is* beautiful"[1]—and attributing that predicate entirely to the subjective reaction in the observer's mind—e.g., "*I have* beautiful feelings when I see the Pietá." (But, as Lewis notes, this account is semantically inept, since the viewer of the Pietá has feelings of "awe" or "reverence" and not "beauty" *per se*.) It is the difference between saying "I prefer freedom over tyranny because it is good," and saying "Freedom over tyranny is good because I prefer it." Although two different speakers may announce to the world that each supports "freedom over tyranny," they may not, at a more fundamental level, be talking about the same thing.

This way of approaching questions of value undermines their objectivity. If the waterfall is not simply sublime in itself, then any judgment of the waterfall's aesthetic quality cannot in principle be wrong. Thus, the person who says that the waterfall is ugly is simply announcing to us his subjective reaction to the cascading H_2O that is appearing before him. However, he is not free to say that this ugly descending liquid is *not* H_2O. For that molecular description is a quantifiable deliverance of the hard sciences. This means that when we look at nature, including human beings, we are limited to explanations that can be measured. Because judgments of quality—including ethical judgments that arise from traditional morality—cannot be appraised by the instruments of the hard sciences, they cannot literally refer to anything real outside of the subjective perception of the one issuing the judgment. There is, then, no evil or good in the world *per se*, but merely a moral interpretation of the world imposed on it by our minds, arising almost exclusively from the emotions, sentiments, and feelings of the interpreters.

For one sort of conservative—the one who is a traditional moralist—the lesson of *The Green Book*, if widely appropriated by one's culture, will lead to the weakening, and perhaps ultimate disintegration, of those institutions, practices, and beliefs that such a conservative believes are essential to the common good. Take, for example, the institution of marriage. Up until just recently, it was uncontroversially believed that marriage is a natural institution, entered into by one man and one woman, who are bound to each other permanently and exclusively, with the begetting and rearing of children as the perfection or natural end of their union. To put it another way, marriage is by nature conjugal, permanent, and exclusive. This was, as Lewis would put it, part of the *Tao* (or the Natural Law), the repository of fundamental truths about the human good that one cannot prove (like when one proves that wine is on the table or water is H_2O), but what one must first believe in order to prove anything else (like when one assumes the reliability of one's cognitive faculties, that truth is better than falsehood, and that other minds exist). It is, in the words of philosopher J. Budziszewski (2011), what we can't not know.[2]

In some Western nations, including the United States and the United Kingdom, the Innovators—as Lewis had called those who want to reason outside the confines of the *Tao*—have largely succeeded over several decades in slowly eliminating from the civil law each element of marriage's nature. With no fault divorce, the cultural debunking of the taboo of extra-marital sex, and the severing of sexual relations from reproduction (what the ancients called its perfection), the philosophical grounds for conjugality have been as good as vanquished for quite some time. Thus, it was a *fait accompli* that same-sex "marriage" (SSM) would become a Constitutional right under American law years before the US Supreme Court issued its definitive judgment in 2015 in *Obergefell v. Hodges*.[3]

But the elimination of marriage's elements would not have succeeded if not for the cultural appropriation of *The Green Book*'s moral subjectivism. If the nature of marriage, like the beauty of the waterfall, is but reducible to our emotions, sentiments, and feelings, then just as one cannot in principle correct someone who says the waterfall is ugly, one cannot in principle judge as non-marital any romantic relationship that its partners choose to call a marriage.

Also essential to the Innovator's project is the denial of final causality, the view that given their nature or form, natural objects—including human beings and their powers and parts—have proper ends to which they are ordered. So, for example, the traditional moralist, when assessing the nature of our sexual powers, argues that they are ordered toward the good of reproduction by means of the real organic unity of complementary spouses. Although pleasure is a desired side-effect of using those powers, that is not *their* point. That, of course, may be the point the participants have in mind. But for the traditional moralist, one's subjective aim for the use of a natural power cannot by itself reveal its proper end. After all, it would not count against the judgment of the traditional gastronomist that one is wrong in eating and puking a Big Mac for sheer pleasure by telling him it was that end that one had in mind. Consequently, the cultural eradication of final causality as a legitimate category of rational deliberation is essential to unencumbering ourselves from the belief that the exercise of our sexual powers ought to be guided by the *Tao*. As Lewis put it: "Now I take it that when we understand a thing analytically [whether sex or eating] and then dominate and use it for our own convenience, we reduce it to the level of 'Nature' [i.e., the categories of the hard sciences] in the sense that we suspend our judgements of value about it, ignore its final cause (if any), and treat it in terms of quantity" (1947, p. 69).

Nevertheless, as Lewis notes, the *Tao* cannot be totally eliminated, since the Innovator's projects cannot even get off the ground without cherry-picking from the very *Tao* he seeks to subdue. This establishes for Lewis his point that though one cannot prove the *Tao*, one needs it in order prove anything else. Consider these two contemporary examples.

(1) In his majority opinion in *Obergefell*, Justice Anthony Kennedy makes his case for SSM, not by "inventing a new value" (1947, p. 44) as Lewis would put it, but by taking "fragments from the *Tao* itself, arbitrarily wrenched from their context in the whole and then swollen to madness in their isolation, yet still owing to the *Tao* and to it alone such validity as they possess" (p. 44). Justice Kennedy writes that "[f]rom their beginning to their most recent page, the annals of human history reveal the transcendent importance of marriage" (*Obergefell*, 2015, at 3). After citing Confucius and Cicero, and acknowledging

how “untold references” to the beauty and grandeur of marriage have been expressed through the ages in a variety of forms and across differing cultures, he concedes that “[i]t is fair and necessary to say these references were based on the understanding that marriage is a union between two persons of the opposite sex” (*Obergefell*, 2015, at 4). He goes on to affirm that “the centrality of marriage to the human condition makes it unsurprising that the institution has existed for millennia and across civilizations. Since the dawn of history, marriage has transformed strangers into relatives, binding families and societies together” (*Obergefell*, 2015, at 8).

Although “the ancient origins of marriage confirm its centrality” (*Obergefell*, 2015, at 6), Justice Kennedy argues that it has developed over time, “even as confined to opposite-sex relations” (*Obergefell*, 2015, at 11). Citing as examples changes in laws on arranged marriages and the role and status of women within society and marriage (*Obergefell*, 2015, at 11–12), he concludes that allowing same-sex couples to marry is just another stage in marriage”s ongoing evolution. Yet, this seems to beg the question, since the developments mentioned by Justice Kennedy were not contrary to the understanding that marriage is by nature conjugal, permanent, and exclusive. So, what maintained continuity through these developments, to use Lewis’ language, was marriage understood from within the *Tao*, and not the “marriage” of the Innovators.

Consequently, in order for Justice Kennedy to claim that “the history of marriage is one of both continuity and change” (*Obergefell*, 2015, at 6), he must first know the nature of the sort of thing that is undergoing the change so that he can distinguish between a real development and a change that breaches continuity. To provide a concrete example, I know that the being that is the acorn that becomes the sapling that becomes the oak tree is one thing that maintains continuity while undergoing change. On the other hand, when I chop down the oak tree and turn it into a desk, there is a breach in continuity—or a substantial change—from which an entirely new thing arises, even though its parts were made from the old thing and could have been used to make something else that superficially resembles the old thing, such as an artificial “oak tree.”

Of course, the story of the oak tree’s development and subsequent destruction is just an analogy. Marriage, like any other apparently natural institution, is not a singular thing, as is the being that is the acorn, the sapling, and the oak tree. Nevertheless, it has a reality that is greater than the sum total of its members, each of which is a particular sort of thing, a human being, which has the capacity to fulfill conditions that make the union a real marriage. This is why, if marriage has a nature, just not any friendship between two or more human beings can count as a "marriage."

Imagine, for example, I tell you that the athletic friendship I have with my basketball buddy, Alden, is a marriage. On what grounds could you say that I am wrong in thinking that athletic friendships could be real marriages? (Saying that the law does not recognize such friendships as marriages simply won't do, since I can merely claim that Alden and I are in the same position as committed gay and lesbian couples before SSM was legally recognized.) You could say that Alden and I do not have a romantic relationship. Although true, that does not seem relevant. Many people marry who do not have romantic feelings for each other, while many people with romantic feelings for each do not marry. What about commitment? It depends what you mean. After all, Alden and I are committed to playing basketball at least twice a week. Suppose you reply, "That's not a life-long commitment." But why should that matter? I have a friend who has committed to caring for his aging parents for the rest of their lives. Is he married to them? On the other hand, as I have already noted, with no-fault divorce, our laws have already jettisoned the condition of life-long commitment. But suppose you say, "What about sexual exclusivity? You and Alden are not having sex. You are only playing basketball." This won't do either. For one reason, our law permits so-called "open marriages," in which sexual exclusivity is actually frowned upon. And secondly, what is sex and why is it so special? It's obvious that sex is a reproductive act. (If not, then why do only those who engage in intercourse use contraception in order to make sex "safe"?) But in that case, because we are both men, Alden and I cannot literally have sex with each other. For even if we achieve orgasm while using our reproductive organs, we are not engaging in a reproductive act, just as I would not be engaging in a nutritional act if I were to use my mouth and stomach to swallow and consume an ashtray.[4] So, it seems we cannot fulfill the sexual exclusivity criterion even if we wanted to.[5] You could, of course, just deny that sex is by nature a reproductive act and say that sex is whatever Alden and I say it is. But by going this route, you have abandoned any principled grounds to say that Alden and I are wrong in claiming that playing basketball is just our way of having sex. In other words, if the nature of sex is just like the sublime waterfall, then it is in our minds and not in the thing that we are describing.

Moreover, if sex is so special for marriage's licitness, and marriage is, as Justice Kennedy puts it, of "transcendent importance," shouldn't the law condemn the extra-marital sex condoned by the wider culture and agree with those who want to legally limit sex to marriage even though they are portrayed in our media as horribly retrograde fun-killing prudes? So, if the law does not recognize sex as special, and our culture treats it as just another form of recreation, why can't Alden and I seal our relationship with a little game of one-on-one, so to speak? If, as Justice Kennedy says in another Supreme Court opinion, that liberty is "the right to define one's own concept of existence, of meaning, of the universe, and of the mystery of human life" (*Planned Parenthood v. Casey*, 1992), then who's to say that basketball is not marital consummation to me and Alden?

But in *Obergefell* Justice Kennedy claims that the "marriage" he is securing in his opinion is in historical continuity with the marriage of the *Tao*, even though each of its three conditions—permanence, exclusivity, and conjugality—have been eradicated from the law and significantly diminished in the culture. It is only by cobbling together accidental features that flow from instances of true marriage and that are also found in some non-marital friendships—fragments of the *Tao*, so to speak—that give Justice Kennedy's understanding the appearance of being in continuity with "the ancient origins of marriage [that] confirm its centrality" (*Obergefell*, 2015, at 6).

Justice Kennedy, for example, points out, among other things, that same-sex couples have romantic feelings for each other,[6] sometimes adopt children for whom they seek legal stability,[7] desire that government ascribe dignity to their unions,[8] and would accrue numerous state benefits as do ordinary married couples if their unions are officially recognized as marriages.[9] However, these accidental features—romantic feelings, children, government recognition, and state benefits—though often accompanying marriage, may in fact be present in non-marital relationships and absent in real marital unions even though one of them, the caring of children, is a proper accident of the marriage of the *Tao* (i.e., a perfection to which one of the essential features of marriage, conjugality, is by nature ordered).[10] For this reason, the principal intuition of one type of conservative—the traditional moralist—is vindicated by Justice Kennedy's

Obergefell opinion: the truths of human nature embedded in the *Tao* are so fundamental to human flourishing that even those who attempt to silence the *Tao* must do so by deploying its moral grammar.

(2) Soon after Pope Benedict XVI announced his abdication of the papacy, the eminent science writer and Oxford professor, Richard Dawkins, sent out this tweet: "I feel sorry for the Pope and all old Catholic priests. Imagine having a wasted life to look back on and no sex" (Dawkins, 2013).

If you know anything about Dawkins, you know that he is the quintessential scientific rationalist, denying that anything that cannot be captured and quantified under the categories of the hard sciences, or traceable to them, is outside the purview of reason—and that anything outside that purview is *de facto* irrational. For this reason, as the Pope Emeritus would have put it, Dawkins has an aversion to asking philosophical questions about the grounds of reason that cannot be subsumed under the rubric of scientific rationalism.[11] As Lewis diagnosed the problem: to suggest that all reason is merely scientific rationality is to sequester oneself from the fullness of Reason, including Practical Reason, the sort of reason that cannot be scientifically proven, but which any scientific proof, or any moral argument that purports to rely on scientific proof, must presuppose.[12]

So let us explore the Reason that dares not speak its name. Dawkins, as is well known, maintains that reason—understood as equivalent to scientific rationalism, which has established the truth of evolutionary theory—requires that we deny that nature is designed, and thus is not infused with final causes (i.e., intrinsic purposes or proper ends) by which we can issue moral judgments.[13]

Setting aside his ungrounded belief that biological evolution *per se* is inconsistent with final causality,[14] it should be clear that Dawkins' scientific rationalism means that his anti-papal tweet cannot be a deliverance of reason. After all, for one to claim that a life of priestly celibacy devoted to Christ and his Church is *a wasted life* requires that one know what a fulfilled life would look like. But such a life is an ideal, and thus is not like an empirical claim about the natural world. It is not an object of scientific inquiry. One cannot point to it, as one would point toward Pope Benedict or Richard Dawkins, though the intellect can be aware of this abstract truth when assessing Benedict and Dawkins by it.

Just as we know that a blind person ought to have sight because we know what a human being is by nature and how his parts and properties are ordered toward certain ends that work in concert for the good of the whole, we also know what excellence and virtue are before and after we see them actualized in our fellows. But given his diminished understanding of reason, Dawkins must deny that even he can issue such judgments by means of his rational powers. As Lewis explains: "The rebellion of new ideologies against the *Tao* is a rebellion of the branches against the tree: if the rebels [like Dawkins] could succeed they would find that they had destroyed themselves" (1947, p. 44). Consequently, on Dawkins' own account of reason, his verdict on the Pope's life is the cerebral equivalent of covert flatulence gone terribly wrong: not silent and not deadly. So, ironically, it is only with fragments of what he has claimed to have debunked, the *Tao*, that Dawkins is able to issue his judgment against the former pontiff. For this reason, just like Justice Kennedy in *Obergefell*, Dawkins cannot escape the perennial truths he claims have been discredited by new insights that our ancient predecessors were not wise or enlightened enough to entertain. For in the process of making his argument, Dawkins must procure the very philosophical resources he claims his argument has made obsolete.

So, there is a type of conservatism—which I call the conservatism of the traditional moralist—that appeals to the normativity of the natural law in the deliberation of our public questions, which is the view Lewis clearly articulates in *The Abolition of Law*. It is a type of conservatism that accepts the truths of human nature as givens that a government cannot ignore in crafting its laws and policies if its end is the common good. It is a type of conservatism that sees the debunking of ordinary common sense intuitions—as we saw in our analyses of both *Obergefell* and Dawkins' mocking of Pope Benedict—as vain attempts to remake or reinterpret the inherited wisdom that is outside the ken of any collection of bureaucrats or experts. This is not to say that the conservatism of the traditional moralist is not open to change or development. Rather, it means that in order to be a genuine development, change must be made within the confines of the *Tao* and justified by how the change advances the *Tao*'s basic goods. As Lewis explains:

> There is a difference between a real moral advance and a mere innovation. From the Confucian "Do not do to others what you would not like them to do to you" to the Christian "Do as you would be done by" is a real advance.

> The morality of Nietzsche is a mere innovation. The first is an advance because no one who did not admit the validity of the old maxim could see reason for accepting the new one, and anyone who accepted the old would at once recognize the new as an extension of the same principle. If he rejected it, he would have to reject it as a superfluity, something that went too far, not as something simply heterogeneous from his own ideas of value. But the Nietzschean ethic can be accepted only if we are ready to scrap traditional morals as a mere error and then to put ourselves in a position where we can find no ground for any value judgements at all. It is the difference between a man who says to us: "You like your vegetables moderately fresh; why not grow your own and have them perfectly fresh?" and a man who says, "Throw away that loaf and try eating bricks and centipedes instead."
>
> 1947, pp. 45–46

But there are other types of conservatism, some of which are not entirely congenial to the reasoning of *The Abolition of Man*. Consider what I call *market conservatism*. This is the view that because free markets have been so efficient and successful in producing wealth and prosperity, and thus allowing us to enjoy many other goods, we should apply the reasoning of the market to all aspects of life. Because the value of commodities is discovered by calculating the price for which people are willing to pay for them, the values of all apparent goods—including those givens of human nature that the traditional moralist believes are objective intrinsic goods and not the product of human will—carry no normative weight whatsoever for the market conservative. As he sees it, these givens, far from being basic truths of human nature on which the common good depends, are constraints on the liberty of each individual to pursue his own subjective vision of the good life. For this reason, for the market conservative, the almost exclusive goal of politics is limited government, by which he means not only a free market economy but also the elimination of laws or customs that interfere with the pursuit of the desiring self. Thus, on this account, the common good (if you can even call it that) is measured by how unencumbered the individual is from tradition, nature, familial ties, religion, etc. to acquire what he wants and when he wants it.

And yet, in practical politics, market conservatives and traditional moralists often find themselves employing similar vocabulary and arriving at similar conclusions on matters of policy, though their underlying rationales are remarkably different. Like the market conservative, the traditional moralist often advances the cause of "limited government." So, for example, both will support a free market economy, since it has the best track record of any system in raising standards of living. But what's the point of raising standards of living? For the market conservative, "to get people fed and clothed is the great end," as Lewis puts it (1947, p. 42). The question of how these people conduct their lives—whether they follow the precepts of natural justice—is outside the law's jurisdiction as long as their conduct does not interfere with the private choices of their fellow citizens to pursue their own visions of the good life. Although the traditional moralist agrees with the market conservative that the acquisition of wealth and being fed and clothed are good things, he views them as worthy of pursuit only because they are connected to one's natural duties to spouse, progeny, neighbor, nation, and God. Thus, for the traditional moralist, liberty is the freedom to pursue the unchosen goods of natural justice unencumbered by external agents, such as criminals or unjust governments. On the other hand, for the market conservative, liberty is freedom to pursue whatever one desires unencumbered by any non-chosen obligations to spouse, progeny, neighbor, nation, or God. For the traditional moralist, the good is what is desirable in itself, while for the market conservative, desiring something is what makes that something good.

So, we are back to the underlying philosophical question in Gaius and Titius' discussion of the waterfall's sublimity: are descriptions of the moral and aesthetic qualities of natural objects (as well as natural institutions that flow from human nature) in the things themselves or just in our minds? But just like that English schoolboy who innocently and uncritically assimilates the *The Green Book*'s answer to that question, most of our fellow citizens who say they believe in limited government have "no notion that ethics, theology, and politics are all at stake" (p. 5).

Notes

1 This is my example, not Lewis'.
2 J. Budziszewski, *What We Can't Not Know: A Guide* (2nd edn., 2011).
3 *Obergefell v. Hodges*, 576 U.S. (2015) (slip opinion).
4 This, by the way, is why the moral traditionalist claims that the intimate relations of a same-sex couple are not ontologically equivalent to the reproductive acts of a

sterile or contracepting male–female couple. The latter, due to natural defect or artificial impediment, cannot fulfill the end to which they are ordered, which is reproduction. The former are not ordered to reproduction because they are not reproductive acts. The moral traditionalist could also put it this way: sterility, whether natural or contrived, is a privation of conjugality, whereas the absence of conjugality is the privation of nothing.

5 I am, of course, not suggesting in this analysis that people who experience same-sex attraction cannot love one another or that their relationships cannot be true friendships. The question explored here has to do with the nature of marriage and not the nature of love or even friendship.

6 "Petitioner James Obergefell, a plaintiff in the Ohio case, met John Arthur over two decades ago. They fell in love and started a life together, establishing a lasting, committed relation" (*Obergefell*, 2015, at 9).

7 "In 2009, DeBoer and Rowse fostered and then adopted a baby boy. Later that same year, they welcomed another son into their family. The new baby, born prematurely and abandoned by his biological mother, required around-the-clock care. The next year, a baby girl with special needs joined their family. Michigan, however, permits only opposite-sex married couples or single individuals to adopt, so each child can have only one woman as his or her legal parent. If an emergency were to arise, schools and hospitals may treat the three children as if they had only one parent. And, were tragedy to befall either DeBoer or Rowse, the other would have no legal rights over the children she had not been permitted to adopt. This couple seeks relief from the continuing uncertainty their unmarried status creates in their lives" (*Obergefell*, 2015, at 10).

8 "No union is more profound than marriage, for it embodies the highest ideals of love, fidelity, devotion, sacrifice, and family. In forming a marital union, two people become something greater than once they were. As some of the petitioners in these cases demonstrate, marriage embodies a love that may endure even past death. It would misunderstand these men and women to say they disrespect the idea of marriage. Their plea is that they do respect it, respect it so deeply that they seek to find its fulfillment for themselves. Their hope is not to be condemned to live in loneliness, excluded from one of civilization's oldest institutions. They ask for equal dignity in the eyes of the law. The Constitution grants them that right" (*Obergefell*, 2015, at 33).

9 "[J]ust as a couple vows to support each other, so does society pledge to support the couple, offering symbolic recognition and material benefits to protect and nourish the union. Indeed, while the States are in general free to vary the benefits they confer on all married couples, they have throughout our history made marriage the basis for an expanding list of governmental rights, benefits, and responsibilities. These aspects of marital status include: taxation; inheritance and

property rights; rules of intestate succession; spousal privilege in the law of evidence; hospital access; medical decision making authority; adoption rights; the rights and benefits of survivors; birth and death certificates; professional ethics rules; campaign finance restrictions; workers' compensation benefits; health insurance; and child custody, support, and visitation rules" (*Obergefell*, 2015, at 21–22) (citations omitted).

10 "Proper accident" refers to those attributes that flow from the nature of a thing, e.g., because human beings are rational animals they are ordered toward the ability to reason, laugh, communicate, etc. But when a human being, because of disability or immaturity, does not exercise these abilities, he does not cease to be a "rational animal." In the same way, as I have already noted in the text above, the conjugality condition of marriage may be fulfilled even if the perfection that flows from the nature of the act is never actualized due to disability or artificial contraception.

11 "The West has long been endangered by this aversion to the questions which underlie its rationality, and can only suffer great harm thereby. The courage to engage the whole breadth of reason, and not the denial of its grandeur—this is the programme with which a theology grounded in Biblical faith enters into the debates of our time" (Pope Benedict XVI, 2006).

12 "All the practical principles behind the Innovator's case for posterity, or society, or the species, are there from time immemorial in the *Tao*. But they are nowhere else. Unless you accept these without question as being to the world of action what axioms are to the world of theory, you can have no practical principles whatever" (Lewis, 1947, 39–40).

13 Writes Dawkins: "The most ingenious and powerful crane so far discovered is Darwinian evolution by natural selection. Darwin and his successors have shown how living creatures, with their spectacular statistical improbability and appearance of design, have evolved by slow, gradual degrees from simple beginnings. We can now safely say that the illusion of design in living creatures is just that—an illusion" (2006, p. 188).

14 See, for example, Etienne Gilson's *From Aristotle to Darwin and Back Again: A Journey in Final Causality, Species and Evolution* (2009).

Works cited

Budziszewski, J. (2011), *What We Can't Not Know: A Guide* (2nd edn.). San Francisco, CA: Ignatius Press.

Dawkins, R. (2006), *The God Delusion*. Boston, MA: Houghton Mifflin Harcourt.

Dawkins, R. (2013), "I feel sorry for the Pope and all old Catholic priests. Imagine having a wasted life to look back on and no sex" [Twitter], February 11. Available at: https://twitter.com/RichardDawkins/statuses/300976272975212544 [accessed May 4, 2016].

Gilson, E. (2009), *From Aristotle to Darwin and Back Again: A Journey in Final Causality, Species and Evolution* (trans. J. Lyon). San Francisco, CA: Ignatius Press.

Hayward, S.F. (2015), "National review: The musical [updated with comment by John]," *Powerline* [online], November 19. Available at: http://www.powerlineblog.com/archives/2015/11/national-review-the-musical.php [accessed May 3, 2016].

Kirk, R. and Schlesinger, A. (1956), "Conservative v. Liberal—A debate," *The New York Times* [online], March 4. Available at: https://www.nytimes.com/books/00/11/26/specials/schlesinger-debate.html [accessed May 3, 2016].

Koons, R. (2000), "An introduction to conservatism" [online], Texas Public Policy Institute, January 15. Available at: http://www.texaspolicy.com/library/doclib/2000-01-15-conservativeprimer.pdf [accessed May 4, 2016].

Lawler, P. (2000), "Francis Fukuyama as teacher of evil," *The Modern Age* [online], 42.1/Winter. Available at: https://home.isi.org/francis-fukuyama-teacher-evil§hash.ZlphMSAI.dpuf [accessed May 3, 2016].

Lewis, C.S. (1947), *The Abolition of Man—Or Reflections on Education with Special Reference to the Teaching of English in the Upper Forms of Schools*. New York: Harper One.

National Review (2005), "The non-fiction 100," *National Review Online* [online], October 19. Available at: http://www.nationalreview.com/article/215718/non-fiction-100 [accessed May 3, 2016].

Obergefell v. Hodges, 576 U.S. (2015) (slip opinion).

Planned Parenthood v. Casey, 505 U.S. 833, 851 (1992).

Pope Benedict XVI (2006), "Faith, reason and the university: Memories and reflections" [online], September 12. Available at: http://w2.vatican.va/content/benedict-xvi/en/speeches/2006/september/documents/hf_ben-xvi_spe_20060912_university-regensburg.html [accessed May 5, 2016].

6

Theology in *The Abolition of Man*

Judith Wolfe
University of St. Andrews

Early in *The Abolition of Man*, Lewis suggests that the doctrine of objective value is related to theology (as to other domains of human conduct): what seems merely like "English prep"—a particular semantic or pragmatic analysis of rhetoric—in fact rests on and inculcates in the pupils assumptions that have implications for ethics, theology, and politics (Lewis, 1947, p. 16).

For the rest of the book, Lewis remains silent about theology. The monotheists' God does not appear in the main text. Theism in general, and Christianity in particular, are mentioned only in lists of traditional moralities (also including classical and oriental) and in the disavowal that "though I myself am a Theist, and indeed a Christian, I am not here attempting any indirect argument for Theism" (p. 61). What he is not attempting, specifically, is an argument from the existence of objective value (or, as Lewis calls it in this book, the *Tao*) to the existence of God—though in several contemporaneous texts, Lewis does just that.

Two arguments for objective value

What does Lewis mean by objective value or *Tao*? It seems to me that he uses the term in two distinct (but, in this book, conflated) senses. The first, general sense is that value terms—above all, the term "good"—are ineradicable. In Lecture 2, Lewis confronts the subjectivist claim that human action, at its most basic, requires no reference to values either in its conception or in its evaluation: that to describe action in value terms is always to impose a secondary, expendable interpretation on a more basic, "scientific" description that remains neutral with regard to values.

Lewis argues that this subjectivist position is incoherent—that it is not only psychologically but also logically impossible to act or describe action without appealing to values or "ends." "The important point" about even overt proponents of moral subjectivism such as the authors of *The Control of Language*, Lewis argues, "is not the precise nature of their end" in writing a textbook on the subject,

> . . . but the fact that they have an end at all. They must have, or their book (being purely practical in intention) is written to no purpose. And this end must have real value in their eyes. To abstain from calling it "good" and to use, instead, such predicates as "necessary" or "progressive" or "efficient" would be a subterfuge. They could be forced by argument to answer the questions "necessary for what?", "progressing towards what?", "effecting what?"; in the last resort they would have to admit that some state of affairs was in their opinion good for its own sake.
>
> 1947, p. 40

The second, stronger sense is the postulate of a positive deposit of laws of conduct and attitude, including the laws of general and special beneficence, the laws of good faith, mercy, and magnanimity, and duties to forebears and posterity.[1] In other words, Lewis argues that *what* people consider "good for its own sake" is as unchangeable as the fact *that* they orient themselves toward a good.

Lewis repeatedly insists that these are axiomatic human laws, which cannot be argued *for*, but can only be argued *from*. What is more, *they* are a seamless garment, which must be accepted in its entirety.

> We must . . . either extend the word Reason to include what our ancestors called Practical Reason and confess that judgements such as *society ought to be preserved* (though they can support themselves by no reason of the sort that Gaius and Titius demand) are not mere sentiments but are rationality itself: or else we must give up at once, and for ever, the attempt to find a core of "rational" value behind all the sentiments we have debunked.
>
> 1947, p. 44

Lewis presents these two versions as the same argument; but it is important to keep them formally distinct, and look at each in turn. (It is also worth noting—and we will return to this later—that the versions show up separately in relation to theology in different contemporaneous texts: the first in "*De Futilitate*" (Lewis, 1967a) and "The Poison of Subjectivism" (Lewis, 1967b), the second in "The Poison of Subjectivism" and *Mere Christianity* (Lewis, 1952).

Since Lewis believes "objective value" in both senses to be something we can only think and act *from*, not argue *for*, he does not, of course, offer any inductive arguments for the existence of objective value. Instead, he makes different types of argument, which take slightly different forms in each case. Lewis' argument for the first version of the argument, as we have already seen, is that thoroughgoing moral subjectivism is self-referentially incoherent. It is impossible to argue against any value except in the service of another. Titius and Gaius cannot rationally oppose the manipulative use of evocative language except by appeal to some other approach that they regard as good. Lewis' argument for the second version is more speculative: denying the laws he has identified makes us incapable of moral reasoning altogether, because they are "axioms of practical reason."

It is worth probing this language a little. Lewis' claim here is best elaborated as a claim about the logic of moral reasoning. Lewis (like most ethical thinkers in history) understands moral deliberation as syllogistic in nature: a general statement (A) and a specific statement (B) yield as their conclusion an act of judgment, choice, or operation (C).[2] For example,

A. The taking of innocent life is evil.
B. This man is innocent.
C. Therefore, I should not take this man's life.

The general statement A is an axiom of this syllogism: it is argued *from* rather than *for*.

Now, it sounds to me as if Lewis is over-blowing this point when he claims that because they are axiomatic for moral reasoning (i.e., for both active moral deliberation and reflective moral evaluation), the laws he has identified cannot be further questioned. After all, the *logical* claim implies merely that for any given practical syllogism, a general statement (A) has to serve as an axiomatic starting point. But as we can see from the illustration I have just given, the fact that a general statement (or "law") has to act, if at all, as the axiom of a syllogism of specific moral deliberation does not mean that it cannot be the conclusion of a syllogism of general moral deliberation, for example:

A. Rational life is of supreme value.
B. What is of supreme value should not be annihilated without grave cause.
C. Therefore, rational life should not be annihilated without grave cause.

What we can see in this second example is that Lewis' insistence that the specific values that he includes in the *Tao*, though they may be axiomatic in *function* in our everyday moral reasoning, are not axiomatic in an absolute sense, but can (and must) be grounded in a more general theory of the good. Practical reason may require the *concept* of "good" to get off the ground, just like theoretical reason requires the concept of "true" to get moving at all: but what falls under the true, or the good, is at least in part open to legitimate discussion.

The natural law

Lewis' claim not only that to act at all is to orient oneself within a system defined, ultimately, by the value term "good", but also that particular values attach to this term necessarily, requires a further argument, which Lewis does not make in *The Abolition of Man* precisely because he does not want to bring theology into the picture. His wish to avoid theological association is signaled already by his choice of the term *Tao* for what is more commonly called "the natural law"—partly, I expect, to avoid the Roman Catholic associations that that term had in the mid-twentieth century, when the natural law ethics of the First Vatican Council were common currency at Roman Catholic seminaries, but were regarded as thoroughly outmoded in academic philosophy and education, where a backlash against G.E. Moore's claims, in *Principia Ethica* (1903), that "good" was a non-natural value that could be discerned intuitively had produced a wave of emotivist theories of moral discourse. (We will return to this later.)

In order to avoid any metaphysical claims about the nature of the world, Lewis contents himself with the epistemological claim that objective value (or the "natural law") is "natural" to humans in the sense that they know it naturally. But, as we have already said, it is difficult for him to show this, beyond the "grammatical" claim that the concept "good" is basic to all human motivation whatsoever. It is worth looking at Thomas Aquinas's classic formulation of the natural law to understand the lacuna here. For Aquinas, the natural law is natural not merely or primarily in the sense that it is naturally known, but in the sense that it encompasses what is natural to man: not merely honesty, magnanimity, etc., but also the goodness of sexual intercourse, food, and hot baths.

Aquinas begins very much like Lewis, with an argument about the basic orientation toward what beings perceive as "good":

> [A]s "being" is the first thing that falls under the apprehension simply, so "good" is the first thing that falls under the apprehension of the practical reason, which is directed to action: since every agent acts for an end under the aspect of good. Consequently the first principle of practical reason is one founded on the notion of good, viz. that "good is that which all things seek after." Hence this is the first precept of law, that "good is to be done and pursued, and evil is to be avoided." All other precepts of the natural law are based upon this: so that whatever the practical reason naturally apprehends as man's good (or evil) belongs to the precepts of the natural law as something to be done or avoided.
>
> Aquinas, 1-2.94.2

The "good" is that which a creature strives after *naturally*. Natures have ends or "goods": "the end of the harpist is to play the harp" (Aquinas, 1.73.1). Without a definition of the nature—and with it, the natural inclinations—of a given creature or artifact, no substantive definition of the "good" can get off the ground. "Since, however, good has the nature of an end, and evil, the nature of a contrary, hence it is that all those things to which man has a natural inclination, are naturally apprehended by reason as being good, and consequently as objects of pursuit, and their contraries as evil, and objects of avoidance" (1-2.94.2). The natural law, with all its particular precepts, is natural because it enumerates simply what is natural to man. "Wherefore according to the order of natural inclinations, is the order of the precepts of the natural law" (Aquinas, 1-2.94.2). This includes, firstly (in common with all sentient beings), "preservation of its own being, according to its nature: and by reason of this inclination, whatever is a means of preserving human life, and of warding off its obstacles, belongs to the natural law" (1-2.94.2). Secondly, in common with other animals, "sexual intercourse, education of offspring and so forth" (1-2.94.2). Thirdly, "according to the nature of his reason", "a natural inclination to know the truth about God, and to live in society: and in this respect, whatever pertains to this inclination belongs to the natural law; for instance, to shun ignorance, to avoid offending those among whom one has to live, and other such things regarding the above inclination" (1-2.94.2).

Aquinas readily admits that although (as he shows in 1-2.76.1, 1-2.90.2) the precepts of the natural law function axiomatically in specific moral syllogisms, many are not "first principles" in an absolute sense. Consequently, although "certain most general precepts" pertaining to the natural law "are known to all" and "can nowise be blotted out from men"s hearts", "certain secondary and more detailed precepts, which are, as it were, conclusions following closely from first principles", "can be blotted out from the human heart, either by evil persuasions, just as in speculative matters errors occur in respect of necessary conclusions; or by vicious customs and corrupt habits, as among some men, theft, and even unnatural vices, as the Apostle states (Romans 1), were not esteemed sinful" (1-2.94.5).

What cannot be blotted out is "the first principle in practical matters, which are the object of the practical reason"; and this is "the last end of human life", which is "bliss or happiness", the principal object of the natural law (1-2.90.2; see also 1-2.90.2 ad 3). This last end—happiness or beatitude—is found in beholding God himself, partaking in his own self-knowledge. The natural law not only inclines us toward this, but is already its beginning: "[T]he light of natural reason, whereby we discern what is good and what is evil, which is the function of the natural law, is nothing else than an imprint on us of the Divine light. It is therefore evident that the natural law is nothing else than the rational creature's participation of the eternal law" (1-2.91.2).

I have argued in this section that without a conception of human nature like that of Thomas Aquinas, Lewis' identification of "good" as an inescapable value term and the particular laws as its invariable content does not work. This is evident in the fact that similar arguments about the inescapability of moral frameworks—but without *substantive* claims about those frameworks—have been developed with great sophistication by the later Wittgenstein (1958, part II, section 11), Alasdair MacIntyre (1967), Charles Taylor (1989, chapters 1–3), Stanley Cavell (1969, pp. 238–266) and others.

The fact that Lewis tries to build his strong claims for a substantive natural law without reference to a good defined by the rational human creature's orientation toward, and participation in, its divine Creator, means, I would argue, merely that he has to substitute some (not explicitly theistic) conception of the good as a quiet basis for his equation of the first and second sense of "objective value." And what kind of conception this is can be seen from the particular examples that he chooses. It is worth remembering here that except in the appendix, Lewis never attempts a list of precepts contained in the natural law in the text. He only chooses some paradigmatic examples. These include natural phenomena such as waterfalls, deeds such as death for one's country, and persons such as children and the elderly. Thus, he argues that a waterfall does not simply educe, but merits a sense of awe in the face of the sublime;[3] that death in battle is "sweet and seemly" regardless of its concrete manifestation; and that infants are "delightful" and octogenarians "venerable" whether or not any particular onlooker is able to appreciate it. It seems to me that Lewis here imports a particular, post-Romantic valuation of nature into a generally Platonic vision of the universe: descriptions of waterfalls as "sublime," and of children as "delightful," appear self-evident, if at all, only to readers after Rousseau, Kant, and Wordsworth.

It might, of course, suffice to show, as Lewis tries to, that a rejection of objective value in his second sense results in practice in the "abolition of man." If it can be shown that a disregard for the values Lewis enumerates leads to complete moral paralysis, then no metaphysical argument is necessary to ground the phenomenological analysis (though perhaps the phenomenological analysis naturally leads to one). But I do not think that Lewis' argument does show this. His dystopian scenario depends only on the "last step" of questioning value altogether, not on the rejection of any particular precept. In fact, the attempt to yoke the general and the particular together leads, it seems to me, to an essential ambiguity in Lewis' argumentation. At times in the book, he argues that it is *impossible* to escape from the *Tao*, and that it is one of the tasks of education—including his own task as an educator of educators—to recall people to the ground they are already standing on. But at other times, he argues that it is possible but highly *detrimental* to step outside the *Tao*, and that it is the task of education to inculcate values that are in real danger of being lost. One corollary of this ambiguity is the uncertain status of the dystopian scenario presented in the third lecture. Is the projected future, in which a subjectivist account of morality has been realized, a live possibility or a *per impossibile* thought experiment?

Objective value and theology: *Mere Christianity* and contemporaneous essays

Unlike in *The Abolition of Man*, Lewis discusses the relationship between objective value and theology explicitly in several contemporaneous works: *Mere Christianity*, "The Poison of Subjectivism," and "*De Futilitate.*" (Note that in "*De Futilitate*" and "The Poison of Subjectivism," it is the first version of his argument for objective value that is at the heart of the matter, while in *Mere Christianity*, it is the second.) In these texts, the relationship between the natural law and God is very similar to that described by Aquinas.

In *Mere Christianity*, Lewis' opening gambit is that the recognition that all humans "know the Law of Nature" and that all "break it" is "the foundation of all clear thinking about ourselves and the universe we live in" (1952, p. 21). All humans are so inalienably beholden to the demands of fairness, honesty, magnanimity, and bravery that they cannot bear simply to break (or be seen to have broken) them, but immediately produce excuses and extenuating circumstances, both to others and to themselves. For Lewis, this phenomenological observation shows that "there is something above and beyond the ordinary facts of men's behaviour, and yet quite definitely real—a real law, which none of us made, but which we find pressing on us" (p. 30). He then correlates this evidence with the two competing views of the nature of the universe: the "materialist view," according to which mind is a by-product of material processes, and the "religious view," according to which "what is behind the universe is more like a mind"—i.e., something with consciousness, purposes, preferences—"than like anything else we know" (pp. 31–32). Because this mind would *direct* the universe, it would not be discoverable as any of the things *within* the universe. It could only appear as something above and beyond these things: as a cause, standard, law or ideal that moves or draws them. And this, Lewis argues, is exactly what we find "inside ourselves": "an influence or a command trying to get us to behave in a certain way" that is not merely identical with the way we naturally behave

(p. 33). In other words, at the opening of *Mere Christianity*, Lewis identifies the innate recognition of standards of fairness, honesty, magnanimity, bravery, and so forth directly with the voice of God "urging me to do right and making me feel responsible and uncomfortable when I do wrong" (p. 34).

Lewis would, of course, readily admit that this way of speaking is an oversimplification, even a distortion. The picture of God intimating his preferences to humans by making them feel uneasy when they do what he dislikes smacks more of a film director cuing ominous mood music when Red Riding Hood veers off the path, or a wife passive-aggressively burning her husband's dinner when he has offended her, than of a transcendent God.

Elsewhere, Lewis gives a different description of the relationship between God and objective value. In "*De Futilitate*" (1967a), Lewis shifts his vocabulary from that of divine communication to that of human participation.[4] Rather than suggesting that God intimates his wishes to humans through their conscience, he now says that human apprehension of moral value participates in reality. The ineradicable habit of assessing human actions or states of affairs in terms of "goodness" or "fairness," Lewis argues, is not merely a secondary, subjective imposition on states or actions that could more fundamentally be described in value-neutral terms, but accurately registers reality, which is at bottom not mindless and impersonal but governed by mind and personality. In "The Poison of Subjectivism" (1967b), Lewis makes the complementary point that "God neither *obeys* nor *creates* the moral law," but, in some sense, *is* that law. "God is not merely good, but goodness; goodness is not merely divine, but God" (1967b, p. 80).

What is at stake?

It is not my aim in this chapter to assess the cogency of what some have called Lewis' moral argument for the existence of God—especially since no such argument is made in *The Abolition of Man*. But I would like to conclude by discussing some of what is at stake in his conception of the relation between the good (which, in some sense, flows out of God's own character) and moral choice.

The moral view underlying the attack on rhetoric in King and Ketley's *The Control of Language* (the book Lewis criticizes under the title *The Green Book*) was influentially described by Alasdair MacIntyre as "emotivism" (1967, ch. 1). To MacIntyre, the rise of emotivism as a theory about the pragmatics of moral judgments was a direct response to the Enlightenment retention of traditional values without the metaphysical foundations of older Christian eras. Nineteenth-century writers, MacIntyre recounts, had jettisoned the scholastic conception of God as well as the implicit authority of revelation, but continued to claim for traditional laws of conduct of an absolute and binding nature, which—philosophers soon perceived—could not be upheld without the older metaphysical basis. Consequently, these newer philosophers argued that statements such as "good" and "right," taking the *form* of absolute statements, in fact served as nothing more than a veneer of respectability for personal preferences. MacIntyre sympathizes with this emotivist analysis as a response to the bankruptcy of Enlightenment value claims. At the same time, he thinks that an emotivist analysis of the use of moral claims is, in the long run, self-undermining: after all, claims of "good" and "right" will only do the job of persuasion for which they are enlisted if most people do not recognize the mere personal preference that underlies them.

The enduring legacy of emotivism, which MacIntyre regards as the still-reigning paradigm of the late twentieth century (in which he writes), is the assumption that the starting point of moral argumentation and decision is, in each person's case, a bare decision for a particular principle, party, class, action, cause or ideal that cannot be further grounded or argued. "All faiths and all evaluations," he summarizes, "are equally non-rational" (1967, p. 26). Human encounters, consequently, are at bottom encounters of competing or contingently cooperating wills, in which each partner is a potential means toward the other's ends. There is no longer a reliable distinction between manipulative and non-manipulative discourse.

Lewis makes a similar observation near the end of *The Abolition of Man*: "A dogmatic belief in objective value is necessary to the very idea of a rule which is not tyranny or an obedience which is not slavery" (1947, pp. 84–85). A parallel passage is found in "Poison of Subjectivism":

> The very idea of freedom presupposes some objective moral law which overarches rulers and ruled alike. Subjectivism about values is eternally incompatible with democracy. We and our rulers are of one kind only so long as we are subject to one law. But if there is no Law of Nature, the *ethos*

> of any society is the creation of its rulers, educators and conditioners; and every creator stands above and outside his own creation.
>
> 1947, p. 79

The antidote against this bare encounter of wills is not merely belief in divine commands. After all, what can be said about competing humans could also be said of God: "every creator stands above and outside his own creation." It is precisely this voluntarist conception of divine command that troubled Lewis about the Christian conception of God before he became a believer; he explicitly rejects it in "The Poison of Subjectivism": "[I]f the good is to be *defined* as what God commands, then the goodness of God Himself is emptied of meaning and the commands of an omnipotent fiend would have the same claim on us as those of a 'righteous Lord'" (1967b, p. 79).

What underlies the difference between an outlook in which ethics ultimately rests on competing wills and one in which humans are oriented toward a common good is, therefore, not the question of God *simpliciter*, but two conceptions of the will, both of which go back to Scholasticism. In the conception dominant until today, that of Duns Scotus, the will is at its most basic a "power for opposites": the nature of the will is not to be moved by any other power, including the intellect, but to choose freely between different or even opposing goods. This is eminently true of God, who could have chosen to decree all things differently than he has in fact done.

For Lewis (following Aquinas), by contrast, the will naturally wills the good, which is nothing other than the form in which the true manifests itself to the will; the achievement of the good equals happiness or *beatitudo*.[5] In other words, the will is the power whose act moves the human being toward the good (or the true) apprehended by the intellect. It is free in two senses: one, in that it cannot be coerced by any external subject; two, in that it chooses freely the course for the attainment of what is perceived as good. The will of God, on this account, rests in the same good toward which humans strive, and communicates that good as love, drawing creatures to participate in his own happiness.

We can thus see that in C.S. Lewis' silent identification of the good as such and the precepts that make up the natural law, "ethics, politics and theology" are indeed "all at stake." His underlying vision is of *goodness* as the "uncreated" "ground of all existence": "not simply a law but also a begetting love, a love begotten, and the love which, being between these two, is also immanent in all those who are caught up to share the unity of their self-caused life. God is not merely good, but goodness; goodness is not merely divine, but God" (Lewis 1967b, p. 80).

I have said nothing about the question of original sin: the human inability, according to Christian tradition, to fulfill the natural law. In *The Abolition of Man* and texts such as "The Poison of Subjectivism" and "*De Futilitate*", this inability plays a subordinate role, and is limited in scope. Indeed, it is central to Lewis' argument that original sin should not hopelessly obscure human *knowledge* of the *good*, only impair the human ability to pursue it. In *Mere Christianity*, it is precisely the (ultimately inescapable) dissonance between the human recognition of the good and their own inadequacy to it that grounds Lewis' argument for Christianity: it is because we make ourselves daily enemies to the good that is also the ground of our existence that we need what Christianity offers, namely forgiveness and grace.

To account for this dissonance, we have to introduce a further twist into the Thomist account of God as goodness that we have pursued here. The fact that humans cannot obey what is directed toward nothing more or less than the fulfillment of their own nature may have two causes: either (as the Reformers argued) their nature is hopelessly impaired, or (as Aquinas argued) humans have a natural end which they cannot naturally attain. This sounds counterintuitive, but is really of one piece with the image of happiness that Aquinas projects. The good is God himself, and communion with God, in which happiness consists, necessarily demands a transcendence of our own nature, that is, "deification." "Man by his nature is ordained to beatitude [that is, deification] as his end," writes Aquinas; but he is ordained to *attain* this end "not by his own strength, but by the help of grace" (Aquinas, 1-2.114.2).[6]

This seemingly paradoxical (even perverse) postulation of a gap between the natural powers and the natural calling of humans, which renders them existentially "incomplete" and thereby opens the possibility of temptation and sin, seems at first sight merely to deny any moral autonomy to humans. In reality, however, this postulation safeguards human dignity and freedom. On the one hand, a *natural* participation in the divine life is incompatible with the real separateness from God implied in our existence as free created beings.[7] On the other hand, the existence of an eternal barrier between God and man which would be implied were we not *called* to such participation is incompatible with the divine love revealed in the Incarnation, which "wishes the eternal good, that is, [God] himself," for the rational creature, and thus draws us "above the condition of [our] nature to a participation in the Divine Good" (Aquinas, 1-2.110.1).

As C.S. Lewis puts it elsewhere: "Our whole destiny seems to lie in . . . being as little as possible ourselves, in . . . becoming clean mirrors filled with the image of a face that is not our own" (1967c, p. 8). When this comes to pass, "each soul, we suppose, will be eternally engaged in giving away [to its fellow-creatures] that which it receives . . . Its union with God is, almost by definition, a continual self-abandonment—an opening, an unveiling, a surrender of itself" (1972, p. 139).

Notes

1 See especially the appendix to *The Abolition of Man*, "Illustrations of the *Tao*."

2 A classic formulation is Thomas Aquinas, *Summa Theologiae*, 1-2.76.1, 1-2.90.2.

3 "*Erhaben ist, was auch nur denken zu können ein Vermögen des Gemüts beweiset, das jeden Maßstab der Sinne übertrifft*" ("The sublime is that, the mere capacity of thinking which evidences a faculty of mind transcending all measure of the senses"); Immanuel Kant, *Critique of Judgement* (1987, §25, p. 106).

4 This is why I think that David Baggett's and Erik Wielenberg's lengthy discussion of Robert Adams's "social requirement theory of obligation" as a strong contemporary version of Lewis' "moral argument for the existence of God" (Bassham, 2015) in some ways distracts from rather than concentrates on Lewis' arguments.

5 Aquinas, 1-2.94.2.

6 The identification of beatitude and deification is most explicitly made in *ST* 1.12.2 and 3.9.3 ad 3.

7 "Natural," in Aquinas's terminology, refers to a capacity that a being has by its own nature, while "supernatural" refers to a capacity superadded to it by external (divine) agency. A "natural" participation in the divine life would require the possession of a divine nature; in other words, it would mean either that man is himself God (which is nonsensical) or that he is merely an "idea in the mind of God" (which is incompatible with Aquinas's ontology). Cf. also Aquinas's remark: "It is as necessary that God alone should deify, bestowing a partaking of the Divine Nature by a participated likeness, as it is impossible that anything save fire should enkindle" (Aquinas, 1-2.112.1).

Works cited

Aquinas, Thomas (1912–36), *Summa Theologiae* (trans. the English Dominican Fathers). London: Burns, Oates, & Washburne.

Bassham, G. (2015), *C.S. Lewis' Apologetics: Pro and Con*. Leiden: Brill.

Cavell, S. (1969), "Knowing and acknowledging," in *Must We Mean What We Say?* Cambridge: Cambridge University Press.

Kant, I. (1987), *Critique of Judgement* (trans. W. S. Pluhar). Cambridge: Hackett.

Lewis, C.S. (1947), *The Abolition of Man—Or Reflections on Education with Special Reference to the Teaching of English in the Upper Forms of Schools*. New York: Macmillan.

Lewis, C.S. (1952), *Mere Christianity*. New York: Macmillan.

Lewis, C.S. (1967a), "*De Futilitate*," in *Christian Reflections* (ed. W. Hooper). Grand Rapids, MI: Eerdmans.

Lewis, C.S. (1967b), "The Poison of Subjectivism," in *Christian Reflections* (ed. W. Hooper). Grand Rapids, MI: Eerdmans.

Lewis, C.S. (1972), *The Problem of Pain*. New York: Macmillan.

MacIntyre, A. (1967), *After Virtue*. Notre Dame, IN: University of Notre Dame Press.

Moore, G.E. (1903), *Principia Ethica*. Cambridge: Cambridge University Press.

Taylor, C. (1989), *Sources of the Self*. Cambridge: Cambridge University Press.

Wittgenstein, L. (1958), *Philosophical Investigations* (trans. G.E.M. Anscombe, ed. G.E.M. Anscombe and G.H. von Wright). Oxford: Blackwell.

7

Science in *The Abolition of Man*: "Can Science Rescue Itself?"

David Ussery
Arkansas Center for Genomics and Ecological Medicine, University of Arkansas Medical School

Introduction

In the midst of the darkness of the Second World War in 1943, three significant events took place. In February of 1943, the physicist Erwin Schrödinger delivered a series of lectures at Trinity College, Dublin, about how life can be explained by the laws of physics and chemistry; this was published in 1944 as the book *What is Life?*, and was inspirational to Watson[1] and Crick a decade later in their work on the structure of DNA. In June of 1943, construction began of the first electronic general-purpose computer (ENIAC—Electronic Numerical Integrator And Computer). These two events set the stage for my area of research and my discussion in this chapter. The third event was another lecture series given in February of 1942—three Riddell Memorial Lectures given by C.S. Lewis at Durham College, and published in book form as *The Abolition of Man* (Lewis, 1973).

I first read *The Abolition of Man* in 1974, along with *That Hideous Strength* (Lewis, 1968). I was fourteen years old, growing up in Springdale, Arkansas. Through these and other works, C.S. Lewis changed my life. Under the influence of Lewis and Mr. Merrifield, my high school chemistry teacher, I graduated high school deciding that I wanted to get my PhD in chemistry, which I eventually did. Although I did not fully understand everything Lewis had to teach me as a young man, after many years, I realized that Lewis believed that it was possible to be a Christian and also a scientist, without having to choose between the two. Lewis taught me that science was worth pursuing, but he also showed me the dangers in using science to debunk values.

Three questions

Because of my fondness for Lewis' books, I happily accepted an invitation to contribute to this book regarding Lewis' view of science in *The Abolition of Man*. I have been tasked with three questions in this chapter: (1) How does Lewis view science? (2) What does Lewis mean by seeking a new "regenerate science"? (3) How can science provide a cure for or prevent Man's abolition? I have thought about this for many months now, and the approach I have decided to take is to first give a background, discussing science and how things have changed since 1943, along with some stories from my own personal experiences as a scientist, and then use this context for a discussion of C.S. Lewis' view of science.

Background

A brief history of molecular biology, materialism, and "science vs. religion"

Although I am neither a "C.S. Lewis scholar" nor "official expert" on the topic of science and religion, since I was about twelve years old, I started collecting books about science and religion. To this day, I still like to read about the history of science, and I now have several bookcases, with more than a thousand books, about the history of science, religion and science, and a large collection of books on biology, heredity, DNA, and genomics.

In broad terms, biology has become "molecular," starting with Watson and Crick in the 1950s. Erwin Schrödinger first proposed that hereditary information might be digital, or an "aperiodic crystal." He used the analogy of Morse code—a series of dots and dashes could encode many different messages. Inspired by this, Watson and Crick proposed that different DNA sequences could encode many different organisms. We still have not fully figured out all of the details, but we now know that biological information is "digital" in the sense that much of what we inherit in terms of physical traits is due to the sequence of DNA that came from our parents. I will talk more about biological information later, but want to set the context of a larger picture.

One could argue that a physical chemical explanation for life is an extension of the materialistic view dating back more than 300 years. Robert Boyle, "the father of chemistry," managed to distinguish chemistry from alchemy, and published *The Skeptical Chemist* in 1661. My background is that of a chemist, and so Boyle is one of my heroes—there's a plaque on a wall in Oxford commemorating the place where Boyle and Robert Hooke did famous experiments. One could argue that chemistry really is a purely mechanical, materialistic view of the world, which permeates our modern society. Thomas Hobbes (also from Oxford University) and others quickly saw a physical explanation for the universe as a basis for materialism, with no need for a belief in God. But Boyle was certainly not a "materialist"—nor from my perspective can any Christian be a pure materialist: how can you believe in Christ or anything outside of nature if nature is all that exists? Boyle strongly disagreed with the materialism of Hobbes, which appeared no different than atheism; Boyle set aside some money to establish a series of lectures after his death, on the relationship between Christianity and our contemporary understanding of the natural world. The first of the "Boyle lectures" was given in 1692 as *A Confutation of Atheism* (Bentley, 1692), and the series has continued off and on for more than three centuries—the lectures are currently being held at Gresham College,[2] Oxford. A recent Boyle lecture, *The Mathematics of Evolutionary Biology—Implications for Ethics, Teleology, and Natural Theology*, was delivered by Sarah Coakley (2016). Like the Boyle lecture series, the controversy between science and religion has also continued within Oxford University since the time of Boyle and Hobbes, through C.S. Lewis and Julian Huxley, down to Alister McGrath[3] and Richard Dawkins.

The importance of stories

Sometimes telling a story can bring home important points through allegory, like the parables that Jesus told. But just as Merlin the magician in Lewis' fiction book is not referring to a "real" person, so some of the stories in the Bible are meant to bring home a point, and not always describe literal, scientific facts. I bring this up here because in our modern society, people often too easily confuse a story or model with reality—I see this often with new PhD students who are learning to speak the language of science and to grapple with scientific models. Science is about making abstractions to model reality—we strive to lesson our ignorance, to learn from our mistakes, and to construct ever better models. But in the end, these are allegories, and the models should not be confused with reality itself.

I see few references to science when I read through *The Abolition of Man*; the book's subtitle[4] implies that the theme of his three lectures (chapters in the book) is mainly reflections on teaching English to young students. However, Lewis says in the preface to *That Hideous Strength* that his point is to tell a "tall story" to flesh out points made in the *The Abolition of Man*.[5] *That Hideous Strength* was written in the same year as *The Abolition of Man*, although the former is a hefty tome of more than 500 pages, and contains much discussion about science and also the "social sciences." I will spend some time looking at *That Hideous Strength* for additional hints about C.S. Lewis' view on science.

How does Lewis view science?

How did Lewis view science, given his commitment to the "doctrine of objective value"? Although little can be found about his views of science in *The Abolition of Man*, it is pretty clear that Lewis believed in an objective reality, apart from our perception of it—for example, electricity and magnetism existed, even before humans observed it. I think Lewis' view of science was along the lines of Plato's allegory of the cave—we see crude images of reality, and from that must build models for what we think to be "real." I also think that Lewis viewed science as being driven by what we do NOT know,[6] and by trying to figure out the best approximation to use for our models—that hopefully would get closer to this "objective reality," but in the end will always only be a model.[7]

Science is modeling an objective, real physical world. Lewis was very supportive of the "hard sciences," like physics and chemistry, although he was skeptical of the "soft sciences," such as sociology. For example, in *That Hideous*

Strength, the "scientific" discipline of the main character (Mark) is sociology. At one point, a chemist named Hingest says to Mark: "There *are* no sciences like Sociology. And if I found chemistry beginning to fit in with a secret police run by a middle-aged virago who doesn't wear corsets, and a scheme for taking away his farm and his shop and his children from every Englishman, I'd let chemistry go to the devil and take up gardening again" (Lewis, 1968, p. 85). It seems that Hingest is being used as a spokesman for the views of Lewis, and that "true science" is about trying to build ever-better models and approximations of an objective reality, and that the "social planners" are not scientists, but rather using science and technology to achieve their own agenda.

I suspect that Lewis often had lunch with a chemist at Magdalen College, which might have been an inspiration for the Hingest character in *That Hideous Strength*. It is likely that faculty often interacted with one another; Magdalen College is quite small—less than 400 students and a small number of faculty. I remember being impressed when I tutored students at Magdalen, and learned that there was a policy of having at least one tutor for every student. Because of the small intimate environment, it seems to me that Lewis probably had regular discussions with science fellows at Magdalen College, and that he had a fairly good understanding of the scientific method.

Science vs. technology

This is probably a kind of technical point, but on the surface, one might have the impression that Lewis has confused science with technology, or at any rate lumped them together. However, I can understand the larger point Lewis was making. Basic research in science is for knowledge, in understanding how things work. Technology is the useful application of this knowledge—for example, in building bridges, or better products. I'm sure that Lewis was well aware of the contrast between the science started with the Greeks, and the technology used by the Romans, who had little interest in science (Russo, 2004). Lewis makes the point in some of his books that many people think that the ancients were kind of dumb, and that with the progression of time, we are much smarter. It is true that with the accumulation of scientific knowledge, there are more facts available to us, but in many ways people today are the same, in terms of capabilities in learning and in basic human behavior, as they were two thousand years ago. Lewis clearly knows a lot about ancient history, because of his extensive classical education and his expertise in Medieval and Renaissance Literature. I was surprised to read a quote from C.S. Lewis in a book on "Myths about Science" that was just recently published; I wonder if Lewis would be bothered by others using him to "debunk a scientific myth."[8]

I am impressed by C.S. Lewis' comments on the use of power in science and technology in *The Abolition of Man*:

> Man's conquest of Nature, if the dreams of some scientific planners are realized, means the rule of a few hundreds of men over billions upon billions of men. There neither is nor can be any simple increase of power on Man's side. Each new power won by man is a power *over* man as well. Each advance leaves him weaker as well as stronger.
>
> Lewis, 1973, p. 58

I agree. Where does this leave us? On the one hand, yes, I think science is great—I love the technology and being able to have iPhones and check my email all the time. But sometimes it is nice simply to get away, and "Be Still, and Know that I am God." This can be difficult to do in a society where we constantly have a screen in our face, interacting with us, demanding our constant attention. I often talk about the explosion of information in my lectures. I tell my students "what information consumes is obvious"—it consumes our attention. Hence a wealth of information means a deficit of attention. We simply get overwhelmed, and sometimes miss the obvious. But there is something else going on here—think of the enormous power that the makers of iPhones have over millions (billions?) of users. Consider the ever-growing power of social media in our lives. Science feeds technology, and it is the application of technology that can vastly empower the few "scientific planners."

Is C.S. Lewis attacking science?

"Nothing I can say will prevent some people from describing this lecture as an attack on science. I deny the charge, of course . . ." (Lewis, 1973, p. 65). Lewis states the foregoing after he says,

> It might be going too far to say that the modern scientific movement was tainted from its birth: but I think it would be true to say that it was born in an unhealthy neighbourhood and at an inauspicious hour. Its triumphs have been too rapid and purchased at too high a price: reconsideration, and something like repentance, may be required.
>
> p. 66

Wow, I'm sure this would offend many modern scientists! But to be honest, I can see where Lewis is coming from here. I think many in our modern society have this kind of blind faith in science (and the Enlightenment). And somewhat ironically, science is now saying that we are not as rational as was assumed in early modern science, several hundred years ago.

Much recent scientific research indicates that we're not nearly the clear thinkers as the Enlightenment assumed—we often get things wrong, make bad decisions, and in general mess things up.[9] From my perspective, realizing this prompts me to be a lot more forgiving and tolerant of others who make mistakes (like me—we all have sinned), but I am sometimes amazed at how intolerant it seems our society has become. We have all seen how a person can make a bad post or link on Facebook or Twitter, and they're haunted for the rest of their lives. I find frightening the machine-learned racism that came out of the "chatbot" Tay, designed for human engagement as part of an artificial intelligence (AI) project (Victor, 2016). At least some people were surprised at how quickly Tay picked up from others and "learned" some pretty depraved ideas. I think Lewis would not be surprised. The problem was not in the actual AI software, but rather what was being used as a training set. This is part of the education of young schoolchildren that Lewis was worried about. Based on *The Abolition of Man*, one could argue that Tay the "chatbot" should first have been given historical stories as a training set—epics and sagas handed down through the ages, coming from the Greeks, Hindus, Norse, Chinese, etc., and from this then been allowed to extract the "*Tao*." Of course, such a trained "moral chatbot" probably would not be very popular amongst youngsters in the "twitterverse." But who knows—some children crave a sense of right and wrong, and are in the process of learning moral values. My point is that the *Tao* exists, but is not easily found in the unrestrained social interactions of young people. Morality is not something that spontaneously appears, but must be learned through positive examples.

I think that in a sense, science has "rediscovered" the total depravity of humans, and at the same time the value in stored wisdom (also known as "religion"). Historically, science was very precise, clockwork, and certain. Now, within the past hundred years or so, modern science has been transformed to being uncertain.[10] But at the same time it has become "less certain," it has become more dominant in society, and now most people assume that science can be the judge of all truth—that is, one can somehow use science to obtain moral values, to provide purpose and meaning in life. Through technology (an application of science), we have now become overwhelmed with "too much information," distracted by what is new and shiny, and seem to have no time for focusing on what is really important. Many of the younger people cannot imagine a time when instantaneous communication and entertainment was not ubiquitous. There have been dramatic changes over the past hundred years.

I remember being surprised when we were looking for a church, after having moved to Oxford, England. A friend of ours from Magdalen College had suggested St. Clements church, and when we asked around for directions, several people told us that it had moved to a "new location." Having moved from Houston, Texas, the "new" church looked quite old. We later learned that the church been built in 1828, but the original parish dated back a thousand years, founded in the year 1004, and got its name from the first recorded rector (Richard de St Clemente) in 1232. "New College" in Oxford was founded in 1379, and the "New Inn Hall" dates to the fourteenth century. Thus, the word "new" had a different meaning at Oxford than in other parts of the world.

In light of this, I remember realizing one day that the science buildings on South Parks Road in Oxford were not really that old (compared to the history of science). Even the "older" buildings were only about a hundred years old, which were "young" compared to many of the other buildings in Oxford. As I began to think about this some, I realized that early on, science was only a relatively minor part of most of the colleges. There is a small "Boyle-Hooke" plaque on High Street, commemorating experiments that Boyle did at University College. But at the time, there was only a few rooms used for science. It is only in the past hundred years or so that science has become a dominant presence at universities. This brings me to some more "stories" that are a bit of a tangent, but provide some necessary background for some points I want to make at the end of this chapter. I want to give a brief overview of how biology has changed since the time of Lewis' writing in 1943, followed by a discussion of how "big data is meeting biology," and then finally come back around to a slightly modified version of the question of "Is C.S. Lewis attacking science?"

What is new in biology since 1943?

In broad terms, looking back over the years, I can see three stages or movements within biology, since the 1940s: first there was molecular biology,[11] which tended to be very reductionist—taking apart things and seeing how they work, and coming up with molecular explanations for biological events. More recently, there has been a trend towards systems biology,[12] which tries to put things back together and model whole "systems" in biology. This is easier said than done, of course, and much of systems biology currently still tends to be from a reductionist point of view. Finally, the most recent trend is a kind of evolution of genetic engineering—now it is becoming possible to design and synthesize new life forms—called synthetic biology, where scientists design and construct living organisms.[13] The idea is that if a person can make it, then they understand it. This can lead to applications that C.S. Lewis imagines might be possible in his writings, such as in *The Abolition of Man*. But to understand this last and most recent trend, I want to first go through the other two.

1. Reductionism—molecular biology—1943-present

My background is as an experimentalist—I was trained as a molecular biologist / biochemist. During my studies in college and graduate school, I became obsessed with DNA and the history of the discovery of genetic material—the "physical basis for life" that Schrödinger was talking about in 1943. "Molecular biology" has at its heart a fairly simple idea, worked out in the 1960s, that DNA encodes genes that are transcribed as messenger RNA (mRNA), and that the mRNA gets translated to proteins. (Or, "DNA makes RNA makes proteins.") This is something that is very basic and is one of the first things taught in introductory biology courses. There are a lot of details here, but the bottom line is that we now understand an amazing amount of the molecular basis for how life works, and this can be reduced to (bio)chemistry and physics. Molecular biology is considered "reductionistic" because the purpose is to decompose or "reduce" all complex biology in the cell down to a set of more tractable chemical reactions. One of the classical questions is "what is the function of this gene?" A simple question, but often we don't know the function, and infer what it does, based on experiments. Imagine a simple genome with 500 genes. One could knock out each gene individually, and then see what happens to the cells.[14] If the cells cannot grow, the gene is said to be "essential" for function. Sometimes biologists get lucky, and find that if a gene is deleted or de-activated, they can observe a particular function.

2. Reconstruction—"systems biology"—1990s–present

More than twenty years ago, when I was a post-doctoral fellow at Oxford University, I was given the first sequence of a bacterial genome, before it was published. I became very interested in this, and a few years later, in 1998, started my own small research group comparing bacterial genomes, at the Center for Biological Sequence Analysis (CBS), in Denmark.[15] At the time, there were only eight bacterial genomes published, and sequencing cost several hundred thousand dollars, and could take a year or longer to complete. Now, sequencing a bacterial genome costs a few dollars, and can be done in a few minutes; we have a collection of more than 70,000 different bacterial genomes, and soon will have more than a hundred thousand. There are a couple of million viral sequences available. The point is, "big data" has come to biology. Many biologists have not fully realized this, and most people in the field are still using methods developed nearly three decades ago.[16] These methods were "cutting edge" at the time, but today the sequence databases have grown more than a quadrillion times larger and the methods still use more or less the same approach.[17] Further, as we've been sequencing more diverse organisms, some of the initial assumptions were found to be not true.

There are two types of problems—at least! First, the "real world" (objective reality, if you will) is much more complicated than assumed; it is now obvious that sequence diversity is far greater than most people thought. Second, what we measure is not as accurate as most people believe; when we observe biological systems, there is a lot of noise—again, much more noise than had been assumed. Mistakes are made, and current technology is simply not adequate to answer basic questions about genome sequence variation, because the read lengths are quite short (a few hundred base pairs), and many genomes have repeats which make mapping those reads back unambiguously impossible. Further, in the biological world, sometimes genes get expressed at the wrong time, or in the wrong way. In short, biology is messier and sloppier than we would like to think. At the molecular level, much of life is driven by "randomness."[18] I think many people have difficulty understanding randomness, and part of this comes from our culture—inherited from the Greeks, who saw randomness as bad, and order as good. But in our world that we inhabit, there is an element of unpredictability, and apparently random events happen, beyond our control.[19] In physics, a table appears to be solid and obeys the predictable laws of Newtonian physics, but when one zooms in to the atomic level, it becomes more probabilistic and less deterministic. In quantum mechanics, strange things happen at the molecular level—or at least strange to us. Molecular biology (as the name implies) is all about modeling events at the molecular level, where things are far more sloppy and messy and not as easy to predict. We can get an average idea of what is going on, but it is important to remember that much of the individuality of organisms has its origins down at the molecular level.

In this context, it is important to think about the general view of science in society, and compare this with "What is Lewis' view on science?" Sometimes I smile when I think about how upset people get when they think someone is criticizing science, and how it works. Of course, there are plenty of "science deniers" out there. But on the other hand, there are also many who think that science can do no wrong. Without being spoken, the underlying assumption in many people's minds is that scientists are very rational people, dealing with pristine, clean data, and a set of rigorous protocols, that will allow for the "truth" to be precisely determined. However, what I see is much muddled thinking, very messy data, and people bumbling around in the dark. In one of his books, Lewis quotes Aristotle: "Those who wish to succeed must ask the right preliminary questions" (Lewis, 1978, p. 1). I was reminded of this the other day, sitting at a meeting where the main person in charge of the project clearly did not know where he was going, or what he wanted to do. His manager asked what he was expecting to publish, and he had no idea, really. Sadly, I see many experimentalists design "fishing expedition" projects where they "hope to find something," without really having thought carefully about what it is they expect to see. Sometimes we have ideas, test them, and get lucky and get a clearer picture of what is going on, and build better models; in general, there is a kind of "consensus" of scientific theory. But as I've said before, what I think drives science is more trying to solve what we do not know, pushing the boundaries. But of course, in order to do this, we must have a clear grasp of what it is that we do know.

I keep telling my students that it really helps to have a clue! With way too much data consuming our attention, we easily get distracted from what is important, and can wind up chasing what is new and shiny, rather than addressing fundamental questions that can test our models—we make predictions, with a clear idea in mind—if I understand this, then I should see this outcome. I think it is important to have a clear model to test. This is different from merely looking at correlations and hoping something might jump out. The latter is useful in biology, but from my perspective, can be dangerous. As just one of many examples, there is a very strong correlation between eating raw tomatoes and being Jewish.[20] But correlation is not the same as causation.

One of my colleagues made the comment that the difference between him and me was that I have a deep knowledge of one area (genomics), and he has knowledge of many different areas. This was really not meant as a compliment,[21] but I think he's right—it is true that I do know an awful lot about one particular area—and I want to take advantage of my "deep knowledge" of genomics to explore the implications of Lewis' view of science.

The "post-genomics" era

In 1995, the first two bacterial genomes were sequenced, with about 1700 proteins encoded by one, and roughly 500 proteins encoded by the second. Comparison of these two genomes yielded about 250 proteins common to the two of them. This was heralded as the set of essential proteins, for all of life. Five years later, in 2000, the number of genomes had increased tenfold (to twenty), and now the set of conserved proteins found in all twenty had dropped to 80 proteins. In 2006, a study of almost 200 genomes found that only 31 proteins were conserved, and a few years later, in 2010, my group found[22] that the number dropped to zero proteins conserved (!) when we looked at a thousand genomes. This simply does not make sense—because obviously one needs the same basic functions across all of life.

Because of this, we started examining the conservation of functional domains, which is a bit of an abstraction, compared to the traditional approach of looking at conservation of the full-length proteins. Early results indicated a set of about a hundred domains conserved across a thousand bacterial genomes, and a few of these domains were of unknown function (DUFs—Domains of Unknown Function). This is kind of fun—there are some functional domains, we haven't a clue what they do, and yet they are found in nearly every single bacterial genome that has been sequenced! At the time of writing, we have examined more than 70,000 bacterial genomes, with a much larger set of more than 15,000 known function domains. We find about 500 functional domains conserved across all bacteria, including a couple of DUFs. These contain all of the basic functions for life—many (~400) for metabolism (to "eat"), with the remainder including all the necessary functions for reproduction (DNA, RNA, and protein synthesis). There appears to be redundancy—that is, in a pinch, some of the domains can substitute for each other, although not as efficiently. But this adds robustness, allowing for bacteria to survive insults from the environment. There is also good experimental evidence from gene knockout studies of about 500 "essential functions" in bacterial genomes, regardless of size, from relatively small genomes encoding less than a thousand proteins, to much larger genomes encoding more than 10,000 proteins. This also provides the basis for designing genomes to use with "synthetic biology"—more on that later in the chapter.

By focusing on an abstraction of proteins (functional domains), this allows us to do very fast searches—for example, we can look for specific functions across a thousand *E. coli* genomes in less than half a second,[23] compared to several weeks using the older full-length alignment approaches. We are working with the computer science group at ORNL to further improve our speed, likely more than a million times faster than traditional methods. Even with this significant increase in speed, it will still take careful planning and critical thinking in order to keep up with the avalanche of new data being generated.

This is a long story, and kind of technical, but there is an important point here: we are viewing the "function" of a protein as an abstraction—by looking for known conserved functional domains, or short amino acid sequence motifs. This greatly speeds things up, but because it is an abstraction, this is an approximation—it gives us a general idea, but when we start looking at the specific details, things get complicated. From my perspective, I really do not think that we can completely understand all of the details of how life works, but we can certainly build some very good models that are predictive of most details. And for most questions asked, these models are "good enough." But we do not yet have complete, robust, definitive models for how life works. This does not mean that we will never get there, just that the problems are complex, and there is a lot we still do not understand. This brings me (finally!) to synthetic biology, where people are trying to literally create new forms of life.

Synthetic biology—2000–present

If you can make it from scratch, then you understand it—this is the idea behind synthetic biology, where one can design and construct novel organisms from a standardized list of parts,[24] and university students can participate in the iGEM (International Genetically Engineered Machine) competition.[25] I have been invited to give talks at meetings on synthetic biology, even though I think this area is not really my area of expertise. In a sense, synthetic biology is partly about engineering organisms, and often people want me to talk about minimal bacterial genomes, that can be used as a "chassis" or starting material for use in synthetic biology. Just last week, I was interviewed by a journalist researching an article on synthetic biology,[26] and this week I've been asked to review another article on synthetic biology and have been invited to write a book chapter on "redefining life."[27] One of my PhD students is currently taking a course on synthetic biology, and is currently working on a list of genes for optimal design for a "streamlined," robust small genome that can be used for synthetic biology. I like the "streamlined" approach, rather than "minimal," because we want something that can grow quickly enough to do experiments, and robust enough to be able to survive and be productive.

About five years ago, I was invited to give a talk in China at a meeting on synthetic biology; I was one of a panel of twelve experts they brought in. The

Chinese want to use synthetic biology in their industry—they have the goal of having 10% of their factories use synthetic biology within the next five years, with the percentage rising in the future. For example, they are interested in designing computers that can fix themselves, and having them self-assemble. The idea is to have a set of chemicals that can be mixed together and, under the right conditions, a computer is formed; this computer could then send back commands to make improved designs—so a computer that can improve itself. Kind of strange! Anyway, this conference was sponsored in part by the Max Planck Society in Germany (most of the scientists attending were from Europe; I came from Denmark, and then there were two other Americans—one from MIT in Boston, the other from Texas). There was a session on "ethics" at the meeting after dinner one evening. There were two talks. The first was by an Austrian group, who showed some clips from Jurassic Park, and said that even though Hollywood thinks scientists are bad, in general scientists can be trusted . . . Then the Chinese head of the Beijing Genomics Institute, the largest sequencing center in the world, gave a talk. He said that China was working toward genetically engineering a "superior race," and that he thought this was a great thing (I heard gasps of "Mein Gott" from the Germans!!!). It was a kind of strange and alarming experience. Many (including the other two Americans) were really upset, one of whom was going to complain to her congressman about it; but I felt like there wasn't much we can do here—we are hugely in debt to China. But it was rather disturbing. So from my perspective, the reason I told this story is to say that, yes, I think that "unregenerate science" can be a big threat to humanity. Having said that, based on past experience and knowing genetics, trying to "genetically engineer a superior race" won't work. But we can really create a big mess trying! I think that this is one possible scenario that Lewis was worried about.

Is C.S. Lewis attacking biology?

I want to come back to a slightly different version of the question "Is C.S. Lewis attacking science," by replacing "science" with "biology" in the question. I have had several friends tell me that they have heard that C.S. Lewis was a "young-earth creationist"—that is, Lewis believed that the world was created less than 10,000 years ago, and that biology has simply got it all wrong here, when it comes to biological evolution. Many years ago I remember being surprised in one of Lewis' essays, where he says that "we must sharply distinguish between Evolution as a biological theorem and popular Evolutionism." Lewis distinguishes Evolutionism as a materialistic philosophy and the basis for atheism for many, from the scientific theory of biological evolution.[28] There has been a recent movement to help biologists and evangelicals talk with each other, and many scientists feel strongly that no, Lewis is not attacking biology. Darrel Falk is a biology professor at Point Loma Nazarene University; he describes how C.S. Lewis influenced him, in his wonderful book, *Coming to Peace with Science: Bridging the Worlds Between Faith and Biology*. The audience of Falk's book is evangelical Christians (mainly in the US) who have been struggling with how to accept the biological sciences. The book has a forward by Francis Collins,[29] and the two of them formed the BioLogos Foundation, which seeks to have a conversation between faith and biology. For the past two years, I have given lectures on introductory genomics at a "Science and Faith" workshop for pastors, held at Gordon College, Massachusetts.

How can science offer a cure for or prevent the abolition?

C.S. Lewis clearly sees potential problems for the misuse of science. But are things really completely hopeless? Is the "abolition of man" inevitable? Lewis imagines a "regenerate science" that could be constructive, redeeming, and beneficial, rather than destructive:

> Is it, then, possible to imagine a new Natural Philosophy, continually conscious that the "natural object" produced by analysis and abstraction is not reality but only a view, and always correcting the abstraction? I hardly know what I am asking for. I hear rumours that Goethe's approach to nature deserves fuller consideration—that even Dr Steiner may have seen something that orthodox researchers have missed. The regenerate science which I have in mind would not do even to minerals and vegetables what modern science threatens to do to man himself.
>
> Lewis, 1973, p. 81

To be honest, I am not sure what Lewis means by "regenerate science" here, but I do know that there is an aspect of science that is driven by a humble search for knowledge and understanding, and that requires monk-like devotion. I can see how that science can be used as a tool—for good as in medical research, as well as for bad things such as designing weapons to kill more people more quickly. I want to make one last digression, one last story, and then come back to the point of "regenerate science."

Big data, artificial intelligence, and *The Abolition of Man*

Although Lewis claimed that science was "born in an unhealthy neighbourhood and at an inauspicious hour," it is interesting to contrast this with the history of "data." In her wonderful book *Big Data, Little Data, No Data—Scholarship in the Networked World* (2015), Christene Borgman points out that the word "data" comes from Latin, and was used in math and theology 500 years ago. "Data" originally meant a set of facts, particularly those taken from scripture. Thus, one could imagine a king wanting to know what to do in a particular situation, and he brings in his counselors, and they present the "data" to him—these are arguments from scripture. It was not until the seventeenth century that the word "data" began to take on the meaning we are more familiar with, but Borgman notes: "Now in its fifth century of use, the term data has yet to acquire a consensus definition." Further, data "are not pure or natural objects with an essence of their own. They exist in a context, taking on meaning from the context and from the perspective of the beholder" (p. 18). In biology, we are drowning in too much sequence data, and in a sense dying of thirst for knowledge of the biological context.

There are several ways to deal with too much data. The first is statistics, which can of course be helpful, and provide a good overview of the data. Visualization is another very important way to deal with too much data, and part of my research over the past twenty years has involved visualization of potential DNA structures along a chromosome, and also comparative genomics, where sometimes we are mapping millions (or more!) of comparisons along the chromosome—all in one figure, mapped along a reference genome.[30] I have a slide I made a few years ago, of a bacterial chromosome, compared to more than a hundred other genomes of the same species. On the slide, I've calculated how long it would take, if one were to look at each comparison, gene-by-gene—there are so many comparisons, at the rate of just looking at one per second, it would take more than two years! And yet, here on a single figure it is possible to get an overview of all the comparisons, and zoom in on the electronic version to examine areas of interest.

The third method is machine learning. I often think that since machines got us into this mess of "too much data"—much of the information that is generated is coming from computers—maybe they can help us learn what is important from the data. There are many different approaches to machine learning, but in general all of these involve trying to "learn" how to classify data—and this is where the training sets and quality of known data becomes really important. One popular method, inspired by biology, is to train artificial neural networks (ANNs); for more than twenty years now, there has been a poster on the wall at CBS of the genetic code, along with the chemical structure of the amino acids. This is from a paper[31] from the center director (Søren Brunak), where an ANN was trained to classify the 61 nucleotide triplets of the genetic code into 20 amino acid categories. The question was, how did the ANN "learn" the genetic code? By watching the choice of weights as the ANN learned to make better predictions, it was possible to dissect information about how the genetic code might have evolved over time. This is kind of technical, but I have been impressed by the thought of gaining useful information from watching how a machine learns things. To learn is to err and err again and less and less and less . . . It is an iterative, training process, and again, one needs to have the right training set.

Artificial intelligence has a surprisingly long history. There are Greek myths about thinking machines. Our brains are designed and optimized for sharing and listening to stories. George Zarkadakis argues[32] that we strive to create artificial intelligence to be more successful—AI will prevent us from making mistakes:

> Artificial Intelligence has the potential to make everyone reach perfection in their personal lives, by always choosing the right partner, profession, job—everything. Hard choices will become less hard. The unquantifiable that defines our moral lives will be quantified, because having the technological means to achieve maximum utility from our decisions will prove too great a

> temptation to ignore. Unchallenged by moral dilemmas, secure in the knowledge that we can do no wrong, we will be in danger of losing the most precious part of our humanity: our humility.
>
> 2015, p. 317

And here is where C.S. Lewis and *The Abolition of Man* come into play again, in my opinion. Many years ago, there was a saying in computer science, "garbage in, garbage out." The real trick is to figure out what is important, in terms of what is used for training. Lewis argues that for grammar school students, the best training set for their "human neural networks" is to give them classical stories—epics, myths, moral stories where the children can learn proper moral behavior; it is not something easy in terms of a short list of things to do—there is a need to train people to be able to decide, in a given context, how to behave properly. It is possible, but not easy, and it takes time. And I am not so sure that AI can really *always* help us make the "right choice" or the "best decisions"—this really depends on a large-scale, quantitative evaluation, and from my perspective a full life explored is difficult to quantitate. But, of course, we can learn to make good choices, and to behave morally and make informed, wise decisions.

Summary

Lewis' view of science is that the physical sciences are attempts to model an objective reality, and that science is merely a tool—it is the potential use of science in social engineering that worries him. Further, it is possible for science to be used in a constructive way to bring a "cure" or a prevention of Man's abolition. The choice is ours, and of course is one that society as a whole will experience. The world seems to be changing ever faster, with increases in technology. But at least for now, we are still using the same basic moral reasoning and capabilities.

I want to end with a few disclaimers. In looking at the outline for this book and also doing a bit of research on books about C.S. Lewis, I realize that there is a large group of people in the US who have dedicated themselves to becoming "C.S. Lewis scholars"—going through everything he's written, and spending their whole lives studying his work. I guess in a way this is no different than historians spending their careers studying Abraham Lincoln. Although I would not consider myself in the same category as these people who have dedicated much of their life to studying his work, as I said at the beginning of this review, C.S. Lewis changed my life, for the better, by giving a solid pointing toward classic thought, literature, and values. Finally, the views presented here are of a single scientist—they are my own, and I've tried to take into account views held by other scientists, but this chapter should not be viewed as any sort of definitive, objective view of "Science in Lewis' Writing." It is one view, and I provide references to many books that I have found useful.

Notes

1 The first chapter in *The Molecular Biology of the Gene* (Watson, 1965) is entitled "Cells obey the laws of physics and chemistry;" the first chapter in my textbook on comparative genomics is "Sequences as biological information: Cells obey the laws of chemistry and physics" (Ussery, 2008a).
2 See Boyle Lectures (2016).
3 McGrath has published extensively, including a number of books about C.S. Lewis.
4 "Reflections on education with special reference to the teaching of English in the upper forms of schools."
5 "This is a 'tall story' about devilry, though it has behind it a serious 'point' which I have tried to make in my Abolition of Man;" from the preface of *That Hideous Strength* (Lewis, 1968, preface).
6 See, for example, Firestein (2012).
7 I recommend Alister McGrath's *The Open Secret: A New Vision for Natural Theology* (2008) for an extensive discussion of this.
8 See Michael Keas's "That the Copernican revolution demoted the status of the Earth," in *Newton's Apple, and Other Myths about Science* (2015), which appears in the section entitled "Medieval and Early Modern Science." Keas states, "The British literary scholar C.S. Lewis summarized the medieval vision of the human place in the cosmos to be anthropoperipheral" (p. 24).
9 For example, have a look at *Thinking, Fast and Slow* by Daniel Kahneman (2013), or for something shorter and more fun, *What Makes Your Brain Happy and Why You Should Do the Opposite* (Disalvo, 2011).
10 See, for example, *From Certainty to Uncertainty: The Story of Science and Ideas in the Twentieth Century* (Peat, 2002).

11 See Judson (1979).
12 See Capra (2014). For a more popular overview, see Noble (2008).
13 See Church (2014).
14 See Lazebnik (2002) on the reductionist approach to molecular biology.
15 www.cbs.dtu.dk
16 BLAST, or "Basic Local Alignment Search Tool," developed by Stephen Altschul and colleagues in 1990 (Altschul *et al.*, 1990), is still used by many people to align sequences—it is an extension of methods developed by David Lipman and William Pearson in 1985 (Lipman and Pearson, 1985). Many of my students were not alive when these papers were published!
17 Some of my friends are really impressed with a new method called "Diamond," published in 2015, which can be either faster than the (30-year-old) BLAST method, or as accurate (but not both!).
18 See, for example, *Life's Rachet—How Molecular Machines Extract Order from Chaos* (Hoffmann, 2012). From the introduction: "This book is a vindication for randomness, a much maligned force. Without randomness, there would be no universe, no life, no humans, and no thought" (p. 7).
19 I discuss this further in Ussery (2008b).
20 See Aschwanden (2016). http://fivethirtyeight.com/features/you-cant-trust-what-you-read-about-nutrition/
21 I am utterly dependent on others, and I know that I cannot possibly master every subject, so I try to surround myself with experts that I can trust and who then work together with me as a team. I am often humbled by the amazing productivity and intelligence and creativeness of the people I work with. I find it easy to follow Jim Watson's advice to "never be the smartest person in the room"!
22 See Lagesen *et al.* (2010).
23 See Cook and Ussery (2013).
24 See Knight (2003) on "BioBricks" and "Cello."
25 See http://igem.org/Main_Page. CBS has had student teams participating in iGEM since 2009.
26 See Singer (2016).
27 The email is from a friend of mine, who is a "lecturer in synthetic biology" at University College, London. Here is the full quote: "In particular, I wondered if you would be interested in contributing a review covering the scientific impact of synthetic biology, particularly covering redefining life/species/GMOs."
28 Here is the full C.S. Lewis quote on "biological evolution vs. Evolutionism":

> The central idea of the Myth is what its believers would call "Evolution" or "Development" or "Emergence", just as the central idea in the myth of Adonis is

> Death and Re-birth. I do not mean that the doctrine of Evolution as held by practicing biologists is a Myth. It may be shown, by later biologists, to be a less satisfactory hypothesis than was hoped for fifty years ago. But that does not amount to being a Myth. It is a genuine scientific hypothesis. But we must sharply distinguish between Evolution as a biological theorem and popular Evolutionism or Developmentalism which is certainly a Myth. Before proceeding to describe it and (which is my chief business) to pronounce its eulogy, I had better make clear its mythical character.
>
> Lewis, 1967, p. 93

29 He is also a C.S. Lewis fan, and the director of the National Institutes of Health.

30 See, for example, figure 5 in Vesth *et al.* (2010), "On the origins of a *Vibrio* species." There are some genomic islands containing sets of genes found only in *V. cholera*, and missing in other *Vibrio* species; these genes encode chitinase, or the ability to live on fish gills, providing a unique habitat.

31 See Tolstrup *et al.* (1994).

32 See Zarkadakis (2015).

Works cited

Altschul, S.F., Gish, W., Miller, W., Myers, E.W. and Lipman, D.J. (1990), "Basic local alignment search tool", *Journal of Molecular Biology*, 215, 403–410.

Aschwanden, C. (2016), "You can't trust what you read about nutrition," *Fivethirtyeight.com* [online], January 26, 2016. Available at: http://fivethirtyeight.com/features/you-cant-trust-what-you-read-about-nutrition/ [last accessed May 31, 2016].

Bentley, R. (1692), *A Confutation of Atheism*. From the Origin and Frame of the World. PART II. A Sermon Preached at St. Martin's in the Fields, November the 7th. 1692. Being the Seventh of the Lecture Founded by the Honourable ROBERT BOYLE, Esquire. London: Printed for H. Mortlock at the Phoenix in St. Paul's Church-yard.

Borgman, C. (2015), *Big Data, Little Data, No Data—Scholarship in the Networked World*. Cambridge, MA: MIT Press.

Boyle Lectures (2016), "The Boyle Lectures" [online]. Available at: http://www.gresham.ac.uk/series/the-boyle-lectures/ [last accessed May 17, 2016].

Boyle, R. (1661), *The Sceptical Chymist: or Chymico-Physical Doubts & Paradoxes*. London: J. Cadwell for J. Crooke.

Capra, F. (2014), *The Systems View of Life: A Unifying Vision*. Cambridge: Cambridge University Press.

Church, G. (2104), *Regenesis: How Synthetic Biology will Reinvent Nature and Ourselves*. New York: Basic Books.

Coakley, S. (2016), "The mathematics of evolutionary biology—Implications for ethics, teleology, and natural theology" [online]. Available at: http://www.gresham.ac.uk/lectures-and-events/the-mathematics-of-evolutionary-biology-implications-for-ethics [last accessed May 17, 2016].

Cook, H. and Ussery, D. (2013), "Sigma factors in a thousand *E. coli* genomes," *Environmental Microbiology*, 15, 3121–3129.

Disalvo, D. (2011), *What Makes Your Brain Happy and Why You Should Do the Opposite*. New York: Prometheus Books.

Firestein, S. (2012), *Ignorance—How it Drives Science*. New York: Oxford University Press.

Hoffmann, P.M. (2012), *Life's Rachet—How Molecular Machines Extract Order from Chaos*. New York: Basic Books.

Judson, H.F. (1979), *The Eighth Day of Creation: Makers of the Revolution in Biology*. New York: Simon & Schuster.

Kahneman, D. (2013), *Thinking, Fast and Slow*. New York: Farrar, Straus and Giroux.

Keas, M. (2015), "That the Copernican revolution demoted the status of the Earth," in R. Numbers and K. Kompourakis (eds.), *Newton's Apple, and Other Myths about Science*. Cambridge, Mass.: Harvard University Press.

Knight, T. (2003), "Idempotent vector design for standard assembly of biobricks." MIT Artificial Intelligence Laboratory, MIT Synthetic Biology Working Group [online]. Available at: http://dspace.mit.edu/handle/1721.1/21168 [last accessed May 31, 2016].

Lagesen, K., Ussery, D.W. and Wassenaar, T.M. (2010), "Genome update: The 1000th genome—a cautionary tale," *Microbiology*, 156, 603–608.

Lazebnik, Y. (2002), "Can a biologist fix a radio?—Or, what I learned while studying apoptosis," *Cancer Cell*, 2, 179–182.

Lewis, C.S. (1967), *Christian Reflections*. Grand Rapids, MI: Eerdmans.

Lewis, C.S. (1968), *That Hideous Strength*. New York: Macmillan Publishing Company.

Lewis, C.S. (1973), *The Abolition of Man—Or Reflections on Education with Special Reference to the Teaching of English in the Upper Forms of Schools*. New York: Macmillan Publishing Company.

Lewis, C.S. (1978), *Miracles*. New York: Macmillan Publishing Company.

Lipman, D.J. and Pearson, W.R. (1985), "Rapid and sensitive protein similarity searches," *Science*, 227, 1435–1441.

McGrath, A. (2008), *The Open Secret: A New Vision for Natural Theology*. Malden, MA: Wiley-Blackwell.

Noble, D. (2008), *The Music of Life: Biology Beyond Genes*. Oxford: Oxford University Press.

Peat, D. (2002), *From Certainty to Uncertainty: The Story of Science and Ideas in the Twentieth Century*. Washington, DC: Joseph Henry Press.

Russo, L. (2004), *The Forgotten Revolution—How Science was Born in 300 BC and Why it had to be Reborn* (trans. S. Levy). Berlin: Springer.

Schrödinger, E. (1944), *What is Life? The Physical Aspects of the Living Cell*. Cambridge: Cambridge University Press.

Singer, E. (2016), "In newly created life-form, a major mystery," in *Quanta Magazine* [online]. Available at: https://www.quantamagazine.org/20160324-in-newly-created-life-form-a-major-mystery/ [last accessed May 31, 2016].

Tolstrup, N., Toftgård, J., Engelbrecht, J. and Brunak, S. (1994), "Neural network model of the genetic code is strongly correlated to the GES scale of amino acid transfer free energies," *Journal of Molecular Biology*, 243, 816–820.

Ussery, D. (2008a), *Computing for Comparative Genomics—Bioinformatics for Microbiologists*. New York: Springer.

Ussery, D. (2008b), "Purpose-driven iPod," *Christian Century* [online], September 23, 2008, pp. 11–12. Available at: http://www.cbs.dtu.dk/courses/genomics_course/Purposedrivenipod.pdf [last accessed May 30, 2016].

Vesth, T., Wassenaar, T.M., Hallin, P.F., Snipen, L., Lagesen, K. and Ussery, D.W. (2010), "On the origins of a *Vibrio* species," *Microbial Ecology*, 59, 1–13.

Victor, D. (2016), "Microsoft Created a Twitter Bot to Learn From Users. It Quickly Became a Racist Jerk," *New York Times* [online], 24 March. Available at: http://nyti.ms/1RjYogc [last accessed 19 September, 2016].

Watson, J. (1965), *The Molecular Biology of the Gene*. New York: W.A. Benjamin.

Zarkadakis, G. (2015), *In Our Own Image: Savior or Destroyer? The History and Future of Artificial Intelligence*. New York: Pegasus Books.

8

The Abolition of Man and British Techno-Futurism

James A. Herrick
Hope College

> Only an International Institute of Evolutionary Research under the most stable of Leagues of Nations could hope to create an artificial man . . . But with sufficient consistency of purpose man could do this . . . Time has created man; man may use time to create man once more . . . We are simply going to allow life to evolve itself under ideal conditions . . .
>
> Whyte, 1927, p. 48

> The new man must appear to those who have not contemplated him before as a strange, monstrous and inhuman creature, but he is only the logical outcome of the type of humanity that exists at present.
>
> Bernal, 1929, p. 42

> It is for the conquest of death: or for the conquest of organic life if you prefer. They are the same thing. It is to bring out of that cocoon of organic life, which sheltered the babyhood of mind, the New Man, the man who will not die, the artificial man, free from Nature. Nature is the ladder we have climbed up by, now we kick her away.
>
> Professor Filostrato in C.S. Lewis' *That Hideous Strength*, 1946

This essay explores the intellectual context of C.S. Lewis' *The Abolition of Man*, and also projects Lewis' concerns forward to our own time to assess the accuracy of his vision. After reviewing the argument of *The Abolition of Man*, I will direct attention to three writers whose futurist ideas were of concern to Lewis. J.D. Bernal, J.B.S. Haldane, and Olaf Stapledon were highly influential in shaping a view of science, the future, and technologically assisted human evolution to which Lewis was responding with no small measure of urgency in the third of his Riddell lectures.

I will argue that *The Abolition of Man* incorporates Lewis' case against a futurist ideology he considered a threat to the Christian worldview and ultimately to the survival of the human race. In *The Abolition of Man*, Lewis anticipates an eventuality that today would be referred by risk management experts such as Nick Bostrom as a pan-generational existential risk—the risk of destroying the entire human race forever (Bostrom, 2002). The essay concludes by asking whether Lewis' concerns about the bio-futurist scientistic ideology implicit in popular works by Haldane, Bernal, and Stapledon were well founded. In answering this question, the essay's final section surveys contemporary Transhumanism, a techno-progressive movement I have been following closely for the past several years. I will argue that this growing international movement manifests in its public rhetoric the very assumptions, aspirations, and agenda of which Lewis warned his readers in *The Abolition of Man*. This analysis raises the question of how, in an age of rapidly advancing biotechnology, Christians should respond to the vision of a technologically re-fashioned human race.

The Abolition of Man

Lewis presented the three lectures making up *The Abolition of Man*—"Men Without Chests," "The Way," and "The Abolition of Man"—as the Riddell Memorial Lectures at the University of Newcastle in February of 1942. In the most discussed lecture, and the one from which the book takes its title, Lewis warned of a coming age in which advanced technologies and educational psychology would allow the alteration of human nature itself. In such an event the subsequent history of the human race would be irreversibly redirected. While this future vision may have appeared fanciful to Lewis' original listeners, his argument merits renewed attention in an era in which human genetic structure can easily be re-shaped using CRISPR-Cas9 technology, and moral sentiments are shaped by prevailing tastes and the narratives of popular culture (see Achenbach, 2015).

Lewis opens his first lecture with a critique of subjective valuation as taught in an upper-form English textbook. *The Green Book*, as he terms it, locates values in individual sensory experience rather than in the external world of objects and phenomena. Such valuation removes the head from the body, the mind from the viscera, creating the unnatural phenomenon of "Men Without Chests." It is through the chest—trained emotions—that reason communicates with the visceral springs of action. Moral conviction alone will not produce moral behavior. Lewis writes, "No justification of virtue will enable a man to be virtuous. Without the aid of trained emotions, the intellect is powerless against the animal organism" (Lewis, 1947, p. 15). Lewis explains:

> The head rules the belly through the chest—the seat . . . of Magnanimity, of emotions organized by trained habit into stable sentiments. The Chest–Magnanimity–Sentiment—these are the indispensable liaison officers between cerebral man and visceral man. It may even be said that it is by this middle element that man is man: for by his intellect he is mere spirit and by his appetite mere animal. The operation of *The Green Book* and its kind is to produce what may be called Men without Chests.
>
> pp. 15–16

Progressive education grounds moral judgments in instinct, denying the existence of the perennial and universal moral law Lewis terms the *Tao*: "It is the doctrine of objective value, the belief that certain values are really true, and others really false, to the kind of thing the universe is and the kind of things we are" (p. 12). Lewis affirms the *Tao* as "the sole source of all value judgements. If it is rejected, all value is rejected. If any value is retained, it is retained" (p. 28).

Of particular concern to Lewis was the tendency to place the survival of the human species—or some modification of the human species—above the rights of any individual human being. Here he discovered a contradiction in the ethics of a particular brand of contemporary futurism:

> What is absurd is to claim that your care for posterity finds its justification in instinct then flout at every turn the only instinct [concern for the individual] on which it could be supposed to rest . . . in the interests of progress and the coming race.
>
> p. 25

To ignore the *Tao*'s affirmation of the individual's value for the sake of protecting the species is to cease to operate morally as human beings, a dangerous step toward the abolition of man.

Lurking in the background of the new subjectivism is a malleable conception of the good. Under the moral regime envisioned in *The Green Book*, definitions of good can be manufactured at will. It may even become possible to imagine a new human race technologically shaped according to such a manufactured notion of the good. The power to shape all subsequent generations of the human race might thus come to reside in the hands of technologists and bureaucratic planners. These elites would possess both an artificial notion of the good, and the technological capacity to fashion a new person. "[I]f any one age really attains, by eugenics and scientific education, the power to make its descendants what it pleases, all men who live after it are the patients of that power" (p. 36). However, despite the futurist vision of a splendid new race, these new creatures "are weaker, not stronger: for though we may have put wonderful machines in their hands we have preordained how they are to use them" (p. 36).[1] In a now famous passage from *The Abolition of Man*, Lewis concludes:

> The final stage is come when Man by eugenics, by pre-natal conditioning, and by education and propaganda based on a perfect applied psychology, has obtained full control over himself. *Human* nature will be the last part of Nature to surrender to Man. The battle will have been won.
>
> p. 37

Lewis' deep suspicion of progressive educational projects, subjective morality, and centralized social planning animates *The Abolition of Man*. In the future he imagines, biotechnologists would treat the human race as their "patient." Lewis casts a dark vision of humanity redesigned by scientific programmers who have stepped outside the *Tao*. Should such a project succeed, every individual human being eventually would reflect in every cell a new nature crafted by the group Lewis terms the Conditioners. The new human nature would mirror a false moral vision founded on instinctive notions of progress and the course of evolution. Lewis wrote, "For the power of Man to make himself what he pleases will be the power of some men to make other men what *they* please" (p. 37). These "man-moulders of the new age will be armed with the powers of an omnicompetent state and an irrepressible scientific technique: we shall get a race of conditioners who really can cut out all posterity in any shape they please" (p. 38).

Morality becomes an educational outcome to be crafted rather than an innate awareness to be refined. The Conditioners can "*produce* conscience and decide what kind of conscience they will produce" (p. 39). Ignoring the *Tao*, they become the self-appointed arbiters of good and bad (p. 39).

> Whatever *Tao* there is will be the product, not the motive, of education. The conditioners have been emancipated from all that. It is one more part of Nature they will have conquered. The ultimate springs of human action are no longer, for them, something given … They know how to *produce* conscience and decide what kind of conscience they will produce.
>
> p. 39

In an effort to illuminate the ideological backdrop for Lewis' argument in *The Abolition of Man*, the following pages overview the thought of three prominent early twentieth-century British techno-futurists with whom Lewis was familiar. Each of these writers promoted ideas that Lewis found threatening to a view of the human race rooted in the *Tao*, and each had taken his case directly to the public through popular books, talks, and essays. Though he was responding to more than the ideas of three contemporaries, the works of Olaf Stapledon, J.D. Bernal, and J.B.S. Haldane caused Lewis serious concern about both the direction of science and the public's willingness to embrace dangerous ideas about the technological future.

Olaf Stapledon

While Lewis respected good scientific work, it is clear from letters, essays, and particularly his three science fiction novels that he also maintained a deep suspicion of scientists who treated extra-scientific philosophizing as an extension of science. The villain in two of the *Perelandra* novels is a diabolical scientist with the suggestive name Weston, while a cabal of ideologically driven scientists works its devilry in *That Hideous Strength*. These are not subtle literary gestures. In a 1943 letter to famed scientist and science fiction author Arthur C. Clarke, Lewis made clear his antipathy to the hubristic "scientism" that was "on the way" in the West. Making reference to his evil physicist Weston in *Out of the Silent Planet* (1938), Lewis wrote: "I don't of course think that at any moment many scientists are budding Westons: but I do think (hang it all, I *live* among scientists!) that a point of view not unlike Weston's is on the way" (Miller, 2003, p. 40). However, "a race devoted to the increase of its own forces & technology with complete indifference to either *does* seem to me a cancer in the universe. Certainly if he goes on his present course much further man can *not* be trusted with knowledge" (p. 40).

Unlike most of his colleagues in the academy, Lewis understood the power of science fiction to shape the public mind. He was particularly concerned about popular fiction's capacity to propagate dubious ideas such as humanity's ongoing evolution and limitless expansion into space. H.G. Wells alone produced dozens of futuristic volumes that envisioned a technologically powerful human race expanding its influence to the corners of the universe. In *Things to Come*, the 1936 movie version of Wells' 1933 novel *The Shape of Things to Come*, the character Oswald Cabal states that human progress knows "no rest and no ending:"

> [Humanity] must go on, conquest beyond conquest. First this little planet with its winds and ways, and then all the laws of mind and matter that restrain him. Then the planets about him and at last out across immensity to the stars. And when he has conquered all the deeps of space and all the mysteries of time, still he will be beginning.
>
> Menzies, 1936

It was another author of science fiction, however, who particularly concerned Lewis, a writer possessing "the most titanic imagination ever brought to science fiction," and one whom Lewis said he could "read with delight."[2] Though Olaf Stapledon (1886–1950) is no longer widely known, he had an enormous impact on science fiction's development. From the 1920s through the 1940s, Stapledon developed a highly original literary sub-genre of science fiction—the history of the future.

Stapledon's vision is clearly evident in *Last and First Men* (1930), a strange and complex chronicle of the distant future told in eighteen stages of human evolution developing over a billion years. While not every evolutionary change involves technological tinkering—nor is every new human species and advance over previous ones—some crucial steps in human development certainly do. As the Third Men seek to create a more advanced human, a division of opinion arises between those who want to create a species with a very large brain, and those who do not. As a result of the conflict, "those who sought to produce a super-brain embarked upon a great enterprise of research and experiment in a remote corner of the planet" (1930, p. 157).

Lewis objected not only to ideas about altering human nature, but about propelling humanity into space for the purpose of conquest as well. In Stapledon he found passages suggesting just such an undertaking:

> [Humankind] might explore and colonize all suitable worlds in every corner of the galaxy ... [They] might achieve intercourse with other galaxies. It did not seem impossible that man himself was the germ of the world-soul, which ... is destined to awake for a while before the universal decline, and to crown the eternal cosmos with its due of knowledge and admiration, fleeting yet eternal.
>
> Stapledon, 1930, p. 223

Humanity is an ongoing experiment in technological self-improvement; advances may be followed by periods of precipitous decline into primitive states, but the trend is toward an improved species. Space was humankind's to exploit. Such visions of technological human enhancement and space colonization concerned Lewis. In the preface to *That Hideous Strength* Lewis states that while he admires Stapledon's skills as a story-teller, he objects to his "philosophy" (1946, p. 7). That philosophy would warrant even the elimination of native species on planets humans wished to colonize. Lewis' concerns about such a vision are portrayed in the rapacious approach of Weston and Divine to the residents of Malacandra (Mars) and Perelandra (Venus).

Like many progressive British intellectuals of his day, Stapledon advocated eugenics (Stapledon, 1997, pp. 145–146). Eugenics will allow us to control our own evolution: "Darwin showed that man is the result of evolution. Others have shown that he may direct his evolution." Stapledon asked, "Why is it sacrilegious to use direct means for the improvement of the human race?" By means of reproductive technologies, "we have been given wherewithal to climb a little nearer to divinity" (p. 147). Stapledon's vision ended in an aggregation of minds functioning as a single super-intelligent entity, a theme he also explored in *Star Maker* (1937). Present humanity is merely "a confused and halting first experiment" (Stapledon, 1930, p. 10), a view that deeply concerned Lewis. A "highly advanced" human from the distant future might say to a present-day counterpart that "the loftier potencies of the spirit in you have not even begun to put forth buds" (p. 15).

NASA historian Steven J. Dick writes that "it is difficult to over-estimate the influence of [Stapledon's] work, especially in Britain" (2001, p. 123). Lewis would have agreed with this assessment. As Franz Rottensteiner summarizes Stapledon's narrative:

> The history of the race continues to reel off until finally Eighteenth Man appears, incorporating the positive features of all previous races to crown the history of Man as the ultimate creation of that spirit which permeates the process of evolution in the universe.
>
> Rottensteiner, 1975, p. 64

Thus, according to another authority, "the ultimate salvation, he reiterates, rests in future man biologically improving the species" (Moskowitz, 1963, p. 274). The impulse to improve the human race through technology was one of Lewis' principal concerns in *The Abolition of Man*.

J.D. Bernal

As noted, Lewis differentiated between science and scientism, the former seeking knowledge of nature, the latter seeking control over nature—especially human nature. Scientism is,

> . . . in a word, the belief that the supreme moral end is the perpetuation of our own species, and that this is to be pursued even if, in the process of being fitted for survival, our species has to be stripped of all those things for which we value it—of pity, of happiness, and of freedom.
>
> Lewis, 1982, pp. 71–72

Scientism attributed a spiritual quality to science—scientists embracing scientism functioned as prophetic visionaries, agents of human transformation.

When Lewis imagined scientism embodied, it is likely that famed Irish scientist and futurist J.D. Bernal (1901–1971) came to mind. Bernal advocated governmental scientific planning, space exploration, and experiments aimed at the technological enhancement of human beings. In books such as *The World, the Flesh and the Devil* (1929) and *The Social Function of Science* (1939), Bernal took his progressive scientism directly to the public. He attracted influential followers; Sir Arthur C. Clarke called *The World, the Flesh and the Devil* "the most brilliant attempt at scientific prediction ever made" [2001, p. 410]. Religion scholar Hava Tirosh-Samuelson comments that Bernal "fantasized about the future where science would transform all aspects of social life and would replace religion as the dominant social force, primarily through the transformation of the human brain" (2011, p. 21).

Bernal was an effective popularizer of scientific ideas, and Lewis was aware of Bernal's popular futuristic book. Bernal described in detail a plan for human space exploration and colonization, sketching the design of a ten-mile wide sphere to be constructed in space of transparent material (Bernal, 1929). His space sphere would provide an entirely self-sustained habitat for human colonists, thus allowing the human race to establish a permanent foothold in space. As noted in our discussion of Stapledon's "philosophy," the prospect of humankind reaching and colonizing other planets preoccupied Lewis. A fallen human race propelling itself into space would only spread the scourge of sin to remote corners of the cosmos.

If Bernal's detailed plans for space were intriguing, his plans for future humanity were chilling. The prototype of a new human would be merely a starting point; evolution would be "superseded" by a program of technologically directed alterations to the human body and mind. Bernal wrote that if humans are to adapt to a rapidly changing physical world, then we "must actively interfere in [our] own making—and interfere in a highly unnatural way" (1929, p. 32). This would mean, among other procedures, radical surgery. However, "the carrying out of these complicated surgical and physiological operations would be in the hands of a medical profession which would be bound to come rapidly under the control of transformed men" (p. 38). Entire bodies might be crafted of "some very rigid material, probably not metal but one of the new fibrous substances." The new bodies "might well be rather a short cylinder." Inside this cylinder "is the brain with its nerve connections, immersed in a liquid of the nature of cerebro-spinal fluid, kept circulating over it at a uniform temperature" (p. 39).

Bernal was particularly interested in alterations to the human brain. As one step toward understanding and improving the organ, he proposed sustaining a living brain without a body: "After all it is the brain that counts, and to have a brain suffused by fresh and correctly prescribed blood is to be alive—to think"

(p. 36).[3] We might communicate with the disembodied brain, for "already we know the essential electrical nature of nerve impulses; it is a matter of delicate surgery to attach nerves permanently to apparatus which will either send messages to the nerves or receive them." Thus "connected up," the brain "continues an existence, purely mental and with very different delights from those of the body, but even now perhaps preferable to complete extinction" (p. 36).

Bernal also envisioned a network of connected minds. "If a method has been found of connecting a nerve ending in a brain directly with an electrical reactor," he wrote, "then the way is open for connecting it with a brain-cell of another person." As a result a "more perfect and economic transference of thought" would be afforded, and thus the "co-operative thinking of the future." Eventually, "connections between two or more minds would tend to become a more and more permanent condition until they functioned as a dual or multiple organism" (pp. 42–43).[4] Death itself "would take on a different and far less terrible aspect," due to its being "postponed for three hundred or perhaps a thousand years ..." The "multiple individual" would in effect become "immortal" through a process of constant transferal of "memories and feelings of the older member" to newer ones (p. 43).

Lewis' character Weston in *Out of the Silent Planet* and *Perelandra* was perhaps based on Bernal. Weston represents a startlingly unrestrained scientism like that espoused by Bernal. Bernal proposed a spherical spaceship, like the considerably smaller sphere Weston creates and employs to journey to Mars and Venus. One scholar has argued that *That Hideous Strength* also satirizes Bernal (Sullivan, 2009). If Weston is a caricature of Bernal, and if the character Ransom (a philologist and university professor) is based on Lewis himself, then the scene in *Perelandra* in which the two fight to the death—Ransom decapitating the devil-possessed Weston with a large, jagged rock—takes on remarkable poignancy.

Tinkering with human nature was, for Bernal, only the beginning of directing the future of human evolution. It was just such tinkering that concerned Lewis enough to imagine a cadre of scientists like Bernal directing the future of the human race from a position outside the *Tao*—a vision that haunts *The Abolition of Man*. Indeed, Lewis' third lecture seems at times a direct response to Bernal's *The World, The Flesh and the Devil.*

J.B.S. Haldane

The 1920s and 1930s in Britain spawned a vigorous progressive scientific movement with a propensity for robust speculation about the near and distant future. I have been arguing that C.S. Lewis was, at least in part, responding to this movement in *The Abolition of Man*. Stapledon was a major figure in British bio-futurism, though he lacked the scientific credentials of Bernal and another distinguished futurist, the famed biologist J.B.S. Haldane (1892–1964).[5] While Haldane cultivated a considerable popular following, Lewis expressed reservations about his influence in a letter to Arthur C. Clarke [Miller, 2003, p. 40].[6] Haldane advocated space colonization, human cloning, ectogenesis (gestation of human embryos outside of a human womb), and technologically enhanced evolution. He predicted the use of pharmaceuticals to enhance physical endurance and even the use of specially formulated perfumes to enhance the sense of smell (Haldane, 1937, p. 301).

In his 1928 collection of essays, *Possible Worlds*, Haldane imagined humanity evolving into "a super-organism with no limits to its possible progress" (1937, p. 304). As a final triumph over nature, augmented human beings conquer space, extending their influence throughout the cosmos and thus propagating and perpetuating the human species indefinitely. As has already been noted, Lewis saw profound danger in

> ... the belief that the supreme moral end is the perpetuation of our own species, and that this is to be pursued even if, in the process of being fitted for survival, our species has to be stripped of all those things for which we value it—of pity, of happiness, and of freedom.
>
> Lewis, 1966, p. 77

Such assumptions slowly "creep in" to public discourse "as assumed, and unstated, major premises" (p. 77).

Haldane and Lewis had a personal exchange over what the biologist took to be Lewis' low view of science and scientists. Lewis countered that Haldane misconstrued his argument: "'Scientists' as such are not the target" (p. 78). The problem was "philosophical, not scientific at all" for, as Ransom says in *Out of the Silent Planet*, "the sciences are 'good and innocent in themselves'" (p. 78). However, "evil 'scientism' is creeping into them" (p. 78). Scientism's religious faith in scientific progress, its tendency to see science as transformative, even redemptive, struck

Lewis as diabolical (p. 79). Scientism would employ technology and centralized planning to master the human race and the cosmos itself, subverting natural law and individual rights in the process. "Under modern conditions any effective invitation to Hell will certainly appear in the guise of scientific planning," he wrote (p. 80). Moreover, the public might just capitulate: "The majority in most modern countries respect science and want to be planned. And, therefore, almost by definition, if any man or group wishes to enslave us it will of course describe itself as 'scientific planned democracy'" (p. 75).

A grave danger is imminent when such planning takes on the moral force of a religion, an eventuality Lewis feared:

> I am a democrat because I believe that no man or group of men is good enough to be trusted with uncontrolled power over others. And the higher the pretensions of such power, the more dangerous I think it both to the rulers and to the subjects. Hence Theocracy is the worst of all governments.
>
> 1966, p. 75

Lewis adds, "And since Theocracy is the worst, the nearer any government approaches to Theocracy the worse it will be. A metaphysic, held by the rulers with the force of a religion, is a bad sign" (p. 76). For scientists, "to be a friend of the World is to be an enemy of God" (pp. 78–79). The enormous power of state-sponsored science wed to an irreproachable ideology of redemptive progress would foment a cultural disaster marked by "the growing exaltation of the collective and the growing indifference to persons." In scientism "the individual does not matter;" only science and its "supreme duty" that "abrogates all ordinary moral laws" (p. 84). Thus, fierce resistance to scientism and its agenda is not merely warranted, but morally required.

Haldane was unbothered by such scruples. He envisioned a day in which children would go through gestation outside the womb, allowing radical control over reproduction. Without such aggressive technological interventions, society will collapse. Technologically directed evolution's goal was a "super-organism" (Haldane, 1937, p. 301). There was "no theoretical limit to man's material progress but the subjugation to complete conscious control of every atom and every quantum of radiation in the universe." Technological progress constituted a new religion unconstrained by the moral order of Lewis' *Tao* and powerfully equipped to take charge of the course of history (p. 304).

Education plays a role in bringing about the new order. In a speech titled *Daedalus* (1923), Haldane sought to reconfigure the relationship between the humanities and science. "I think that the blame for the decay of certain arts rests primarily on the defective education of the artists," he wrote (1923, p. 7). In a properly ordered society, art serves science. "Competent" artists are the sort that grasp the goals and methods of science and "understand industrial life." Haldane argued that "if we want poets to interpret physical science . . . we must see that our possible poets are instructed, as their masters were, in science and economics" (p. 7). "The classics" were not of the same value as science. "I am absolutely convinced that science is vastly more stimulating to the imagination than are the classics" (p. 7). Nevertheless, an understanding of literary technique might be of use to scientists. Their best ideas "do not normally see the light" largely because "scientific men as a class are devoid of any perception of literary form" (p. 8). Some appreciation for the techniques of literature would allow scientists to be more persuasive.

Lewis found *Daedalus* chilling, even before his conversion to Christianity. On February 20, 1924, at age 25, Lewis wrote in his diary: "I began to read Haldane's *Daedalus*—a diabolical little book, bloodless tho' stained with blood" (Lewis, 1991, p. 287). Twenty years later his revulsion at Haldane's futuristic vision is still apparent in *The Abolition of Man.*

Transhumanism and the posthuman vision

Stapledon, Bernal, and Haldane represented for Lewis a dangerous version of techno-futurist experimentation unrestrained by the transcendent moral standards of the *Tao*. The three writers thus provided part of the intellectual context in which Lewis operated as he crafted the lectures that would become *The Abolition of Man.* The stakes could not have been higher: the fate of the human race hung in the balance.

Did Lewis have anything to be concerned about? That is, *were* writers such as Stapledon, Bernal, and Haldane prophets of a new human order? This section surveys Transhumanism, a techno-progressive movement that is gaining influence and that espouses goals Lewis cautioned readers of in *The Abolition of Man.* I will note similarities in contemporary Transhumanism and Lewis' dark vision of one possible technological future. Transhumanists speak confidently of achieving goals such as technological immortality, creating computer deities, and radically altering the human race through technological enhancements including genetic and nanotechnological interventions.

While the technologies to bring about his feared future did not exist in the 1940s, the philosophy that would support a brave new world did. Today the technologies also exist. A wide range of organizations currently promotes a philosophy of enhancement, as well as an array of augmentation procedures that raise serious ethical questions. Among the groups backing components of the enhancement vision are Singularity University in California, the Future of Humanity Institute at Oxford University, the Association for the Advancement of Artificial Intelligence in Palo Alto, the European Union's Human Brain Project, the Institute for Ethics and Emerging Technologies, Strategies for Engineered Negligible Senescence (SENS) Research Center, the Methuselah Foundation, Terasem, and many others.

Oxford University's Nick Bostrom, co-founder of the World Transhumanist Association and head of the Future of Humanity Institute, captures the movement's fundamental orientation:

> Transhumanists view human nature as a work-in-progress, a half-baked beginning that we can learn to remold in desirable ways. Current humanity need not be the endpoint of evolution. Transhumanists hope that by responsible use of science, technology, and other rational means, we shall eventually manage to become posthuman, beings with vastly greater capacities than present human beings have.
>
> Bostrom, 2003a

The question of altering human nature—or whether such a nature exists—has emerged as an important topic in bioethics, biotechnology, philosophy, and religion.[7] The prospect is treated by some enhancement advocates as a moral obligation, albeit one developing outside the moral system Lewis termed the *Tao*. The present human is not the crown of God's creative work, merely an evolutionary step toward the posthuman. Transhumanists speak confidently of humans merging with machines and of depositing human consciousness in devices that will render future human species immortal. Stapledon, Bernal, and Haldane had imagined all of this, and their vision alarmed Lewis.

One prophet of the techno-future writes of a "postbiological world" in which humanity will develop in "many novel directions, as each individual mutates by dropping unneeded traits and adding new ones from the growing data banks" (Moravec, 1988, p. 125). Tirosh-Samuelson, a critic of Transhumanism, identifies in the Transhumanist vision specific goals evident in *The Abolition of Man*, including humans working to "redesign themselves" and "also to redesign future generations ... ." Posthumans will "possess new physical and cognitive abilities, and will be liberated from suffering and pain due to aging and diseases" (Tirosh-Samuelson, 2011, pp. 19–20).

Bostrom agrees: humans will "live much longer and healthier lives" and will "enhance our memory and other intellectual faculties" as well as "refine our emotional experiences and increase our subjective sense of well-being, and generally achieve a greater degree of control over our own lives." For Bostrom, enhanced humans of the near future "are much smarter than us ... are much more brilliant philosophers" and will "create artworks, which, even if we could understand them only on the most superficial level, would strike us as wonderful masterpieces" (2003b, pp. 494–495).

Bostrom repudiates claims that such aspirations amount to "playing God, messing with nature, tampering with our human essence, or displaying punishable hubris" (2003a, p. 4). Moving society toward accepting the posthuman will not occur without a contest. Thus, according to sociologist James Hughes, "the human race's use of genetic engineering to evolve beyond our current limitations would be a central political issue of the next century" (2004, p. xii). Nevertheless, human enhancement visionary Ray Kurzweil is confident that technology with soon allow us to "reprogram the information processes underlying biology," essentially altering human nature (Koepp, 2016).

Lewis warned of a technological caste that would take control of human evolution and direct the process toward an end of its choosing. While few concerns are currently raised in enhancement circles about which individuals would be in charge of developing the new humans, or which moral framework would guide these decision-makers, such matters are at the heart of Lewis' argument in *The Abolition of Man*. The Transhumanist narrative has at this point in its trajectory taken on a religious quality that also would have concerned Lewis. As Tirosh-Samuelson writes, "In the posthuman age, humans will no longer be controlled by nature; instead, they will be the controllers of nature" (2011, pp. 19–20).

The scope of research related to human enhancement is incomprehensibly vast and accelerating at a rapid rate. Hundreds of university and corporate research facilities around the world are at work on artificial intelligence, life-extension strategies, human–machine interfaces, and pharmaceutical enhancements of cognitive performance. Transhumanist organizations promote space colonization and support cryopreservation of the dead for later revival or therapy. The collective financial and intellectual clout of all related projects is beyond calculating. A synthesis of scientific culture's most robust metaphysical ideas—progress, evolutionism, the power of information—Transhumanism urges the technological conquest of intractable impediments to human progress: death, space, and human nature. The movement reflects techno-futurist pronouncements about triumphant humanity common in Lewis' day, and ones of which he was keenly aware when writing *The Abolition of Man*. However, an important change has occurred since Lewis' day: the power to transform humanity at the genetic level is now in our hands.[8]

Conclusion

From *The Green Book* to the Conditioners and the loss of the human race in three lectures—the leap is almost too great to provide Lewis a plausible premise for his argument. Surely he had more on his mind in penning *The Abolition of Man* than the moral implications of progressive textbooks. I have argued that he had a particularly influential and hazardous brand of British bio-futurism in view as he wrote, an ideology that preoccupied him and that he also attacked in the Ransom trilogy. Stapledon, Bernal, and Haldane were, for Lewis, prophets of the near future if science accepted their vision.

Lewis wrote of science: "Its triumphs may have been too rapid and purchased at too high a price: reconsideration, and something like repentance may be required." A "regenerate science" would "buy knowledge at a lower cost than that of life" (1947, p. 49). "But," he added, "if the scientists themselves cannot arrest the process before it reaches the common Reason and kills that too, then someone else must arrest it" (pp. 49–50). Such statements are hardly expressive of a concern for *The Green Book*; they are a call to arms in response to a dangerous ideology. In *The Abolition of Man*, Lewis challenged a deified science, driven by a corrupt philosophy and taking human nature as its patient. He wrote to save the human race from such a fate.

I have argued that Lewis was prophetic as regards the advent of techniques powerful enough to bring about the effects he feared. I have also contended that a scientistic philosophy propelling contemporary calls for unhindered biotechnological research currently contributes to conditions that may encourage misappropriation of enhancement technologies. The only remaining question is whether, or perhaps when, such technology will be used to bring about the ends Lewis feared.

A clash of two religious worldviews is in the offing: Judeo-Christian theism and Transhumanist techno-futurism. Religious traditionalists will not readily accept a biotechnological project aimed at creating new human beings at the expense of human nature, and human enhancement advocates—building on the work of earlier visionaries such as Stapledon, Bernal, and Haldane—will not yield their vision of a posthuman future to the objections of opponents they dismiss as bio-conservatives. If Lewis is right in *The Abolition of Man*, this will be a battle for the future of the human race itself. I am convinced he is right. Moreover, one side in the contest is preparing itself for a long cultural struggle, developing its resources, crafting its arguments, honing its public case. The other side has yet to realize that a battle is looming.

Lewis concludes *The Abolition of Man* with a surprising discussion of magic in the Renaissance. He famously referred to the two enterprises as "twins," born at the same time and under the same circumstances. Magic eventually died, but science grew and flourished. Both, nevertheless, were seeking the same ends:

> For magic and applied science the problem is how to subdue reality to the wishes of men: the solution is a technique; and both in practice of this technique, are ready to do things hitherto regarded as disgusting and impious—such as digging up and mutilating the dead.
>
> Lewis, 1947, p. 48

The technological magicians are with us, better equipped, better funded, and more widely supported than they were in Lewis' day. *The Abolition of Man* remains a timely warning.

Notes

1 The idea of technologically improved human beings had been addressed in popular fiction well before Lewis gave his Riddell Lectures. See, for example, H.G. Wells, *Food of the Gods* (1904) and Philip Wylie, *Gladiator* (1931).
2 Sam Moskowitz (1963, p. 261); Lewis (1947, p. 25).
3 Lewis parodied this proposal in a memorable scene from *That Hideous Strength.*
4 This vision of connected minds forming a worldwide "noosphere" had already been explored by writers such as Teilhard de Chardin and Vladimir Vernadsky.
5 For a good introduction to Haldane and his cultural context, see Hughes (2008).
6 See, for example, his letters to Arthur C. Clarke in Miller, ed. (2003).
7 See, for example, *Beyond Humanity? The Ethics of Biomedical Enhancement* (Buchanan, 2011) and *Human Enhancement* (Bostrom and Savulescu, 2011). Savulescu holds the Uehiro Chair in Practical Ethics and is Director of the Oxford Uehiro Centre for Practical Ethics. Bostrom is Director of the Future of Humanity Institute at the University of Oxford. Criticisms of human enhancement include Michael Sandel's *The Case Against Perfection: Ethics in the Age of Genetic Engineering* (2009); Nicholas Agar's *Humanity's End: Why We Should Reject Radical Enhancement* (2010); and Michael Hauskeller's "Reinventing Cockaigne: Utopian themes in Transhumanist thought" (2012).
8 See, for example, Haroon Siddique, "British researchers get green light to genetically modify human embryos" (2016).

Works cited

Achenbach, J. (2015), "Scientists debate the ethics of an unnerving gene-editing technique," *The Washington Post* [online], December 1. Available at: https://www.washingtonpost.com/news/speaking-of-science/wp/2015/12/01/historic-summit-on-gene-editing-and-designer-babies-convenes-in-washington/ (accessed December 7, 2015).

Agar, N. (2010), *Humanity's End: Why We Should Reject Radical Enhancement.* Cambridge, MA: MIT Press.

Bernal, J.D. (1929 [1970]), *The World, The Flesh and the Devil.* London: Jonathan Cape.

Bernal, J.D. (1939), *The Social Function of Science.* Hertford UK: Stephen Austin and Sons.

Bostrom, N. (2002), "Existential risks: Analyzing human extinction scenarios and related hazards," *Journal of Evolution and Technology*, 9 (1).

Bostrom, N. (2003a), "Transhumanist values," in F. Adams (ed.) *Ethical Issues for the 21st Century* [online], Philosophical Documentation Center Press. Available at: http://www.nickbostrom.com/ethics/values.html [accessed May 5, 2016].

Bostrom, N. (2003b), "Human genetic enhancements: A Transhumanist perspective," *Journal of Value Inquiry*, 37, 493–506.

Bostrom, N. and Savulescu, J. (2011), *Human Enhancement.* Oxford: Oxford University Press.

Buchanan, A.E. (2011), *Beyond Humanity? The Ethics of Biomedical Enhancement.* Oxford: Oxford University Press.

Clarke, Arthur, C. (2001), "A Choice of Futures," in Greetings, Carbon-based Bipeds: Collected Essays, 1934–1998, ed. I.T. Macaulay, NY: St. Martins, Griffin, pp. 410–415.

Dick, S.J. (2001), *Life on Other Worlds: The Twentieth-Century Extraterrestrial Life Debate*. Cambridge: Cambridge University Press.

Haldane, J.B.S. (1923), "Daedalus, or science and the future: A paper read to the Heretics, Cambridge University," NY: E.P. Dutton and Co., 1924.

Haldane, J.B.S. (1937), *Possible Worlds*. London: Chatto & Windus.

Hauskeller, M. (2012), "Reinventing Cockaigne: Utopian themes in Transhumanist thought," *The Hastings Center Report*, 42 (2), pp. 39–47.

Hughes, J.J. (2004), *Citizen Cyborg: Why Democratic Societies Must Respond to the Redesigned Human of the Future*. Cambridge MA: Perseus Books.

Hughes, J.J. (2008), "Back to the future: Contemporary biopolitics in 1920's British futurism," *European Molecular Biology Reports*, 9, S59–S63.

Koepp, S. (2016), "Ten questions for Ray Kurzweil," *Time*, *Time* Interview [online], February 3. Available at: https://www.youtube.com/watch?v=0BUYbEgOZt4 [accessed May 5, 2016].

Lewis, C.S. (1938), *Out of the Silent Planet*. London: John Lene.

Lewis, C.S. (1946 [1967]), *That Hideous Strength: A Modern Fairy-Tale for Grown Ups*. New York: Macmillan.

Lewis, C.S. (1947), *The Abolition of Man—Or Reflections on Education with Special Reference to the Teaching of English in the Upper Forms of Schools*. New York: Macmillan.

Lewis, C.S. (1966), "A reply to Professor Haldane," in *Of Other Worlds* (ed. W. Hooper). San Diego, CA: Harcourt Brace World.

Lewis, C.S. (1982), "A reply to Professor Haldane," in *On Stories and Other Essays on Literature* (ed. W. Hooper). Orlando, FL: Harcourt Brace Jovanovich.

Lewis, C.S. (1991), *All My Road Before Me: The Diary of C.S. Lewis 1922–1927* (ed. W. Hooper). London: Harcourt Brace Jovanovich.

Menzies, W.C. (dir.) (1936), *Things to Come*. Movie (United Artists).

Miller, R.W. (ed,) (2003), *From Narnia to a Space Odyssey: The War of Ideas between Arthur C. Clarke and C.S. Lewis*. New York: I Books.

Moravec, H. (1988), *Mind Children: The Future of Robot and Human Intelligence*. Cambridge, MA: Harvard University Press.

Moskowitz, S. (1963), *Explorers of the Infinite: Shapers of Science Fiction*. Westport, CT: Hyperion Press.

Rottensteiner, F. (1975), *The Science Fiction Book: An Illustrated History*. New York: Seabury Press.

Sandel, M. (2009), *The Case Against Perfection: Ethics in the Age of Genetic Engineering*. Cambridge, MA: Harvard University Press.

Siddique, H. (2016), "British researchers get green light to genetically modify human embryos," ***The Guardian*** [online], February 1. Available at: https://www.theguardian.com/science/2016/feb/01/human-embryo-genetic-modify-regulator-green-light-research [accessed May 5, 2016].

Stapledon, O. (1930 [2008]), *Last and First Men*. Mineola, NY: Dover.

Stapledon, O. (1937), *Star Maker*. London: Methuen.

Stapledon, O. (1997), "The Splendid Race," in *An Olaf Stapledon Reader*. Syracuse, NY: Syracuse University Press.

Sullivan, D. (2009), "C.S. Lewis' satirical portrait of J.D. Bernal's *The Social Function of Science*," paper presented at the 95th meeting of the National Communication Association, Chicago, IL, November.

Tirosh-Samuelson, H. (2011), "Engaging Transhumanism," in G.R. Hansell and W. Grassie (eds.) *Transhumanism and Its Critics*. Philadelphia PA: Metanexus Institute, pp. 19–52.

Wells, H.G. (1904), *The Food of the Gods and How it Came to Earth*. London: Macmillan.

Wells, H.G. (1933), *The Shape of Things to Come*. New York: Macmillan.

Whyte, L.L. (1927), *Archimedes or The Future of Physics*. New York: E.P. Dutton and Co.

Wylie, P. (1931), *Gladiator*. New York: Alfred A. Knopf.

9

Metaphors of Meaning: The Dance of Truth and Imagination in *That Hideous Strength*

Scott B. Key
California Baptist University

Abstract

The Enlightenment Project, an intellectual endeavor that seemed to be reaching its apex during the heyday of Logical Positivism in the mid-twentieth century, fundamentally changed the intellectual landscape of the West. Over the course of nearly 400 years, Western thought nearly succeeded in severing the classical and medieval understandings of the inherent connections between (1) fact and value, (2) truth and meaning, and (3) reason and imagination. In the hands of the Enlightenment Project, *value* is reduced to feeling, *meaning* is defined as solely empirically derived truth, and *imagination* is relegated to personal taste and pleasure. C.S. Lewis' *The Abolition of Man*, published in 1943, is a substantial critique of these three critical shifts of the Enlightenment Project; its aesthetic fulfillment followed just two years later in fictional format as the climactic novel of the Ransom trilogy. In *That Hideous Strength*, Lewis powerfully demonstrates the way *values* uncover the significance of facts, *meaning* transforms brute facts into truth, and *imagination*, informed by truth, sharpens the focus of reason.

Introduction

Although it is not "fashionable" in the larger discipline of literary criticism, this essay will assume some interpretive merit in the assertion by C.S. Lewis that the novel *That Hideous Strength* is a narrative expression of the central thesis of *The Abolition of Man* (Lewis, 2003, p. 7). The more germane question is this: in what way or ways does the philosophical/meta-ethical argument of *The Abolition of Man* find expression in the stunningly creative climax of the Ransom trilogy? This chapter will limit the scope of the exploration to two main sub-questions: what is the central argument of *The Abolition of Man* and are there examples or occasions or metaphors within the novel where aspects of the argument are imaginatively expressed? To that end, this chapter can be understood as a dialogue between the philosophical analysis and its imaginative expression. Within each section, the main argument of *The Abolition of Man* will be explored, and specific examples of how the argument is expressed within the genre of imaginative literature suggested. The novel is multi-layered and complex. Many different features of the novel could be used to demonstrate the connection between the two works but only a few need to be suggested in order to establish the thesis.

The Abolition of Man is an exercise in meta-ethical reasoning. Meta-ethics seeks to reflect upon the nature of ethical thought and provide careful analysis of that process. What are the best approaches to the ethical task? What are the implications of one approach over another? Are there central issues related to the character of value, the epistemological access to knowledge of the Good, or to the processes of ethical decision-making that favors one approach in ethical reasoning over another? What are the assumptions that shape, if not govern, the way any theory proceeds to decision-making and are these assumptions viable? These are the questions, along with others, that attend the task of meta-ethics.

Lewis addresses a series of interrelated philosophical and ethical questions central to the debates of the mid-twentieth century whose educational, social, and political expressions are, it is argued, potentially devastating to the further development of Western civilization. From the vantage point of seventy-five years after the publication of these essays, it is clear that Lewis is prescient indeed.

The Enlightenment Project reached its apex in the mid-twentieth century. The assumptions of the Enlightenment thinkers come to fruition in the philosophy of logical-positivism, the subjectivism and emotivism of consequentialism, the eugenics of social Darwinism, and the pervasive material naturalism of scientism. Without tracing the historical expressions of each of these ideas or movements, the inner dynamic of this set of complex ideas can be summarized in three fundamental concepts that mark the severing of the modern from its medieval roots.

First, facts are knowable through our senses and, in some ways, can be asserted as true or false, while values are subjective emotions that are neither true nor false. Second, truth is reducible to facts that have some utility for the human project but the meaning of that project is, at best, a projection of human wishes only tangentially related to truth claims. The third concept is closely tied to the first two. If values are fundamentally "non-sensical" and meaning is merely the projection of idiosyncratic "wishes," then imagination is severed from any relationship to reason and, as such, is unable to provide a vision of universal goodness, truth, or beauty. The isolated individual is reduced to particular self-consciousness, the immediate occasion, the impulsive will, and the impersonal forces of a blind natural process. Such is the modern condition. "Value" is reduced to emotive sentiment, "meaning" is defined as solely empirically derived truth, and "imagination" is relegated to personal taste and pleasure.

The opening scene in *That Hideous Strength* reflects all three of these Enlightenment assumptions enumerated in outline above. Mrs. Jane Studdock is vaguely and almost absentmindedly repeating the definition of marriage adapted from *The Book of Common Prayer* (1559) and used by the priest in her wedding service. The fact that her kitchen is clean and "tidy" and her housework finished lies in stark contrast (in her mind) to the assertion that marriage is ordained for "mutual society, help, and comfort that one ought to have of the other" (Lewis, 2003, p. 11). The "facts" of her life with Mark lie in stark contrast to the "value" the solemnization of matrimony places upon it. The modern emphasis upon "being in love" as an expression of emotion overshadows all assertions of its transcendent value. In Jane's mind the "facts" of her discontent make the "end" or goal of marriage impossible. "Mutual society, help, and comfort" are, seemingly, unrelated and fanciful "ends" to a reality whose meaning is wholly tied to her emotive valuation of her present condition. This deep internal conflict also renders her efforts to understand the spiritual sensuality of John Donne's celebration of our embodied existence impossible. Her dissertation research and writing are as stymied as her celebration of matrimony. Such is her situation. The severing of fact and value, truth and meaning, and reason and imagination has rendered her incapable of entertaining an "enthusiasm" for either John Donne's poetry or for Mark's presence in her life. The use of the word "enthusiasm" by Lewis (pp. 11–12) is directly connected to its etymology. She is no longer "possessed by a god" or experiencing "supernatural inspiration" (*Oxford English Dictionary*, 1989, Vol. V, p. 296). As the novel unfolds, it becomes clearer and clearer that the dichotomies of contemporary culture can only be overcome by an inspiration whose source is God.

The argument of *The Abolition of Man* seeks to make the case for the educational and social implications of these philosophical developments. Lewis calls thinking people to recognize the threat present in the "modern" project. It is a project that undermines the very center, or heart, of what it means to be human. In part one, Lewis addresses the implications of severing fact from value. In the second address, he analyzes the "innovator's" reductive project that takes a portion of the "*Tao*" and, based upon the innovator's instinct, develops this new "foundation" as the basis for a revolutionary vision of human life. This is an exploration of the relationship between truth and meaning. In the last essay, the analysis of the claims of the "conditioner" provides the test case for proposing the return to a renewed understanding of the fundamental connection between reason and imagination. The meta-ethical analysis developed by Lewis is a powerful call to reclaim a vision of reality rooted in an objective moral law and to embrace a virtue-shaped lifestyle that is essential to human flourishing.

Fact and value

It is important to note that Lewis begins the first lecture in *The Abolition of Man* with a discussion of the way *The Green Book* interprets the word "sublime." This very important word is at the center of a long discussion in Western thought of the nature of art and beauty, value and imagination, and fact and reason. This discussion was given its modern flavor by Kant.

Kant reduces the concept of the sublime to a certain kind of judgment that is not a "cognitive judgement" or "logical judgement" but an "aesthetic one" whose basis is "subjective" (Kant, 1952, §1.476). Furthermore, the sublime is distinguished from the mere beautiful. The beautiful is concerned with the "form of the object" and is a "presentation of an indeterminate concept of understanding" (§23.495). The sublime, on the other hand, is marked by "limitlessness" and "quantity" and is a "presentation of the indeterminate concept of reason" (§23.495). Kant argues that the beautiful only describes an individual's subjective reaction to works of human art but connects the sublime to the objects of Nature. Further, the assertion that a natural object is sublime is not a reference to the object in question but is rather a reference to the contents in the mind for "... what is sublime, in the strict sense of the word, cannot be contained in any sensuous form, but rather concerns ideas of reason, which, although no adequate presentation of them is possible, may be excited and called into the mind by that very inadequacy itself which does admit of sensuous presentation" (§23.496).

Despite the "limitlessness" of the idea of the sublime, it is a feature of the natural "rule of ends" of the "whole mechanism" of nature which exhibits the rational maxim: "everything in the world is good for something or other; nothing in it is in vain; we are entitled, nay incited, by the example that nature affords us in its organic products, to expect nothing from it and its laws but what is final when things are viewed as a whole" (§67.559). Kant, in this way, produces a discrete division between the natural sciences whose task it is to study the teleology of the mechanisms of nature and the discipline of metaphysics (and to a much lesser degree theology) whose purpose is to explore the human as a "moral agent" under "moral laws" as the final "end" of creation. This metaphysical reality, for Kant, provides the only clue to the existence of God (§84.587–588).

The result of the Kantian analysis is a bifurcated vision of the world where the *a priori* structure of the human mind "constructs" the contours of our experience of the phenomenal world and the sense of the moral "ought" and the vague and subjective experience of the "sublime" are the only intimations one can have of a reality that transcends our individual understanding.

In the first chapter of *The Abolition of Man*, Lewis criticizes Gaius and Titius for asserting that the use of the word "sublime" is only the utterance of subjective feelings. This not only violates the clear meaning of the word "sublime," it, more importantly, communicates to the schoolboy that all value language is "contrary to reason and contemptible" (Lewis, 2001, p. 9). This is not only bad literary criticism, it is, more importantly, a rejection of the classical understanding of the primary educational task. This task, Lewis asserts, is to introduce and illustrate the "doctrine of objective value, the belief that certain attitudes are really true, and others really false, to the kind of thing the universe is and the kind of things we are" (p. 18).

The center of the lecture is just this: a particular human being can become truly human only to the extent that the "chest" or the "center" or the "heart" of the person is shaped by virtue, by the *Tao*, and is able, thereby, to shape and temper both the appetites and the reason so that behavior begins to align with that which is true and honorable (pp. 23–26). The linkage of "Chest–Magnanimity–Sentiment" (p. 25) by Lewis is important. The "Chest" is the center or the heart of the person. Magnanimity is the characteristic virtue of the "great-souled" person in Aristotle's *Ethics*, which, along with "phronesis" or practical reason, embodies all of the virtues (Aristotle, 2002, *Nicomachean Ethics*, 1123b–1125a, 1140a, 1145a). Lewis uses the word "sentiment" in the sense of "intellectual or emotional perception" and a right "mental attitude of approval or disapproval" (*Oxford English Dictionary*, 2nd edition, Vol. XIV, p. 993) or, in other words, as a synonym for virtue. This use of the word is very close to the Biblical concept of "heart," which is the seat of will and wise decision-making. A person in which these virtues are not developed is a "man without a chest" (Lewis, 2001, p. 25).

The narrator of *That Hideous Strength* (Lewis) illustrates an alternative understanding of the sublime from that provided by Kant. In a visit to Bracton College he, the narrator, was allowed to explore Bragdon Wood for an hour without interference. Each step back to the Wood is a step back in time to a "holy of holies" (Lewis, 2003, p.18). He moved from the Enlightenment scientism of Newton back to the "medieval College." Here the grass is greener and even the old stone buttresses seem alive. The chapel is close at hand and the "hoarse" sounds of an "old clock" penetrates the silence (p. 18). Through this smaller quadrangle called "the Republic" (possibly a reference to Plato"s *Republic*), he passed the "slabs and urns that commemorate the dead Bractonians" and then he moved down the steps into the "full daylight" of the "quadrangle called Lady Alice." The symbolism is powerful. Each step back in time is a step toward the light. "Lady Alice" is a humble "Protestant world," patterned after Renaissance notions of the primitive church, filled with sounds of water and the "cooing of wood pigeons" (p. 18). With a reference to Bunyan, the narrator leads us through a "wicket" across the "fellow's bowling green" to the "high wall of the Wood" (p. 19). He entered the Wood through the only gate and a half a mile further arrived at the centre of the Wood—a well known as "Merlin's Well" with its British-Roman pavement. Here is the center. Here he remembers ancient texts, acts of courage, poets, and "the air was so still and the billows of foliage so heavy above me, that I fell asleep" (p. 20). This is "Faerie" and this is the sublime.

In stark contrast, the rest of the novel provides many examples of the modern, subjectivist understanding of the sublime. One of the more subtle examples of this is illustrated in an event in the small town of Cure Hardy. At this point in the narrative, Mark Studdock is trying hard to get into the "inner ring" of N.I.C.E. (National Institute of Co-ordinated Experiments). After frustrating efforts to gain knowledge of a coherent job description or even to determine his immediate supervisor, Mark is relieved to be given something to do. He and a man named Cosser are to visit Cure Hardy and write a report justifying the destruction of the town that will be caused by N.I.C.E. when a river is re-channeled through it.

Our narrator remarks that "Mark was not as a rule very sensitive to beauty, but Jane and his love for Jane had already awakened him a little in this respect" (p. 84). The drive to Cure Hardy and the walk around the town brought Mark face to face with real people in a real village. The "winter morning sunlight" affected him, the earth and sky "had the look of things recently washed," and the laborer, the pauper, the elderly *rentier*, and the postman evoked memories of a "holiday." "For that reason he felt pleasure in it" (pp. 84–85). Despite its beauty, despite the reality confronting him, despite the pleasant faces and voices, Mark's sociological convictions were unchanged. As he remarks, concerning the whole village: "that sort of thing has to go" (p. 86). His academic discipline had made the "things he read and wrote more real to him than the things he saw" (p. 85). In a sudden insight Mark realizes that Cosser was a person with narrow interests incapable of appreciating anything around him and "what a terrible bore this little man was . . ." (p. 86). Yet Mark is unable to grasp that the pleasure he felt was rooted in reality and reason and that the world he constructed in his mind was not so rooted. Mark is suffering the impact of the separation of fact and value. He is unaware that his love for Jane, which was awakening his capacity for wonder, the capacity for an imaginative appreciation of and openness to the sublime, is directly related to the pleasure he experienced in the village. He is unable to acknowledge that he had been "taught" to disregard or acknowledge the beauty of the "winter morning sunlight" (p. 84) and for that reason he could coldly calculate the destruction of this village in the name of progress. In this simple scene, Lewis illustrates the implication of the subjectivism of *The Green Book*. Mark is becoming "a man without a chest."

When fact is severed from its essential connection with value, two related but different implications immediately arise. First, as Lewis argues, the language of value becomes subjective and non-cognitive. That is, values are understood only to reflect the mental or emotional state of the speaker (the subject) and thus the language provides information only about the subject but provides no knowledge about the object of the language. To state that the waterfall is pretty, in this context, only communicates the subjective attitude of the speaker and provides no information about the reality of the waterfall. All the language of value used in ethical and aesthetical judgment is reduced to subjective or emotive utterances whose truth-value is based solely on whether or not these statements accurately reflect the inner subjective life of the speaker.

Second, this condition also strips the value from statements of fact. This implication is more difficult to describe but it is an equally important corollary to the first implication. If statements of fact are reduced to utterances that neither place value on "objects" outside of our self-consciousness nor render those "objects" as having value themselves, then, eventually, the significance of "facts" as "facts" is lost. They cease to tell anyone anything about reality. Reality as something outside of my self-consciousness soon loses all importance. Lewis provides a perfect example of what happens when facts lose all value to a person and reality becomes more and more imprecise and lost in "fog." That example is Mr. John Wither, Deputy Director of the N.I.C.E. In Mark's first meeting with Wither, Mark endeavors to discover what he might do at N.I.C.E. This conversation is fraught with ambiguity and confusion. The hilarity of the encounter only heightens the reader's suspicion of the Director's disassociation from any normal understanding of reality. Everything is fluid, nothing is concrete, and all is in the "mist:" the job description and expectations; the salary; the beginning of employment; the supervisor; and the mission of the organization (pp. 50–53). Mark's continuing attempts to determine his "status" from the Director and others are frustrated at every point. Mark's situation and the actual condition of N.I.C.E. is symbolized when Mark looks outside a few days later and discovers, "... the fog was thick, wet, and cold" (p. 106).

If everything is reduced in significance, if all value is relegated to an individual's emotional mood swings, then our capacity to locate the contours of reality and determine the nature of truth and meaning is lost in a fog of relativism and solipsism. In such a world the sublime is hidden, the multi-dimensional nature of reality is obscured, the community of truth is lost in the mist, and the "man without a chest" is wandering in the darkness.

Truth and meaning

In an obscure but very significant essay "Bluspels and Flalansferes: A Semantic Nightmare," published in 1939, Lewis examines the nature of language and metaphor. His analysis produces the following conclusions. All language is metaphorical (Lewis, 1969, p. 261). In some uses of language, the metaphors that are employed by imagination to identify and highlight meaning are self-conscious metaphors created by master teachers to help students grasp the meaning of "something" before them. Most of the time, the metaphorical nature of language is hidden or "buried" in the words that are presumed to be literal and free of all metaphor. In these cases, we only fool ourselves into believing that our language is only conveying empirical fact (pp. 259–260). In the most important language, the language of meta-narrative and myth, the meaning is in the metaphors and cannot be extracted from them. One must enter into the metaphors in order to begin to see the presence of meaning at all (pp. 262–263). It is the role of imagination, informed and shaped by virtue and values (the "chest"), that is the creative source of metaphor in and through which we can recognize meaning lying before us. Once the "meaning," made possible by imagination, lies before us, reason can begin the process of determining the truth or falsity of the field of meaning. Reason, then, is the means by which we determine and assign truth-value to the meaning-laden and imaginatively enlivened events, experiences, and discoveries of our lives. Lewis concludes the essay with these significant words:

> But it must not be supposed that I am in any sense putting forward the imagination as the organ of truth. We are not talking about truth, but of

> meaning: meaning which is the antecedent condition both of truth and falsehood, whose antithesis is not error but nonsense. I am a rationalist. For me, reason is the natural organ of truth; but imagination is the organ of meaning. Imagination, producing new metaphors or revivifying old, is not the cause of truth, but its condition.
>
> 1969, p. 265

This theme is explored in the second lecture in *The Abolition of Man*. Lewis argues that Gaius and Titius must have had an "end" or "purpose" for their book. The end or purpose must have "real value in their eyes" but the philosophical position supported by their analysis of value makes that purpose only emotive and, ultimately, meaningless (2001, p. 28). In effect, they are blind to the "background values of their own which they believe to be immune" from their critique of all values (p. 29). Eventually, the "Innovator" is driven to assert that the "core" of traditional values is something more basic than reason or communal flourishing or love for others. Lewis writes, stating the position of the Innovator (the authors of *The Green Book*): "The preservation of society, and of the species itself, are ends that do not hang on the precarious thread of Reason: they are given by Instinct" (p. 33).

This leads to "an infinite regress of instincts," all at "war" with themselves, which we must obey without any standard of judgment that is above that which must be judged (p. 35). As Lewis clearly states:

> If we did not bring to the examination of our instincts a knowledge of their comparative dignity we could never learn it from them. And that knowledge cannot itself be instinctive: the judge cannot be one of the parties judged; or, if he is, the decision is worthless and there is no ground for placing the preservation of the species above self-preservation or sexual appetite.
>
> p. 36

To assert that self-preservation is the basic instinct and that a person must "obey Instinct" provides no grounds for either the past or the future, that is, no grounds for the assertion that one must respect one's parents or plan for the preservation of one's children or grandchildren (pp. 37–38). The effort to invent new values is merely the selection of some values over other values, which "are themselves derived from the *Tao*" (p. 41). The severing of truth and meaning renders both the individual and the society incapable of making reasoned judgment between competing values and claims of meaning. It also reduces human behavior to the instinctual level, which makes self-consciousness and reason impossible. In this address, Lewis builds upon his understanding of meaning, anticipates his defense of miracle, and proves to be a prescient predictor of the consequences of materialistic naturalism and of our contemporary confusion. In 2012, Thomas Nagel put it this way:

> If we were not inclined to recognize objective reasons for action, and were motivated exclusively by our desires, we would have no reason to believe in the existence of value in a realist sense . . . In brief, value is not just an accidental side effect of life; rather, there is life because life is a necessary condition of value.
>
> 122–123

Truth requires the presence of meaning about which rational judgments, rooted and guided by virtue-shaped reason, can be made. If truth is not the result of a rational assessment of the "meaning" that lies before us but only the blind product of instinctual processes, then truth is ultimately a meaningless concept signifying nothing. In the end, the human project is merely survival devoid of purpose.

Returning to the opening scene of the novel, Jane Studdock is struggling with the meaning of her life. The words of the marriage liturgy "stuck in her mind" but the meaning of marriage and the veracity of these words remain a mystery and a source of dis-ease (Lewis, 2003, p. 11). As far as she is concerned, "mutual society, help, and comfort" were not part of her reality (pp. 11–12). The deeper dimensions of the meaning of marriage lie at the heart of this novel. Monika Hilder argues persuasively that the domesticity of the novel is its deepest insight: "the victory of matrimony in the Studdocks' lives . . . deposes scientism from its throne" (Hilder, 2013, p. 84).

But, in addition to this struggle, Jane is experiencing a series of deeply troubling dreams that surprisingly and terrifyingly come true. Her notions of truth and reality are continually upset and overturned. Step by step she is led out of the fog to St. Anne's-on-the-Hill and a meeting with the Director (or Ransom, the Pendragon) (Lewis, 2003, p. 116–135). In this encounter, Jane hears for the first time that marriage is larger than she ever thought. The cosmic is revealed in the domestic. The willingness to die to self and the choice to be obedient to an eternal order means that we must all surrender a "masculine" pride by joining the "dance" of humility that "is an erotic necessity" (p. 146). This truth is embedded in a deeper reality: "... you do not fail in obedience through lack of love, but have lost love because you never attempted obedience" (p. 145). Such obedience alters everything and it is fleshed out in the metaphor of dance (p. 147).

The Director offers Jane a larger and more encompassing field of meaning and a new metaphor by which it can be understood. Immediately, she begins to think about this new meaningful context. As the presence of a transcendent reality begins to come into the Director's rooms, he gently orders Jane to leave and, when she does make her way to the railway station, "she found that, even down there, the fog had begun to lift" (p. 147). The challenging words of the Director begin to alter Jane's understanding of reality. The meaning of her life is reshaped by a deeper truth that begins to realign the context of her being. Her reason assesses the truth-value of this new and deeper metaphorical understanding of reality and thus the door is open to a new reconciliation. Jane's experience includes a new horizon of meaning captured in an imaginative metaphor that challenges the reductionism of mid-twentieth-century thought.

It is crucial to note that the center of the change this new metaphorical understanding of reality brings lies in personal encounter. The meeting with the Director took place in a room filled with light and warmth (p. 139). The first moment she looked at the Director "her world was unmade" (p. 139). The Director seemed to embody and unify a whole set of apparent contradictions: young and old; tranquility and pain; Arthur and Solomon; king, lover, and magician; "battle, marriage, priesthood, mercy, and power" (p. 140). Again, Lewis emphasizes, "her world was unmade; she knew that" (p. 140). The Director then spoke and his voice struck Jane "like sunlight and gold" not just as beauty and gentle light but with heaviness or gravitas and the burning light of the desert (p. 140). And for the third time, in this same scene, Lewis writes: "For her world was unmade: anything might happen now" (p. 141). The three-fold repetition, the juxtaposition of apparently conflicting ideas, and the personal authority of the Director creates the context in which the metaphors of meaning are expanded and reshaped. Truth and meaning begin to dance.

Reason and imagination

The early nineteenth-century rise of Romanticism is, in part, an effort to challenge the growing domination of the Enlightenment vision of reality. It is the argument of Malcolm Guite that the Romantic poet and critic Samuel Taylor Coleridge, in counter-distinction to the Enlightenment Project, develops a Trinitarian understanding of the imagination. This repositions the concept of the sublime from the subjective expressions of the *a priori* reason to a more vivid and compelling symbol of reality (Guite, 2012, pp. 146–147). Guite writes concerning Coleridge:

> . . . Coleridge found himself compelled to reject the mechanistic, clockwork cosmos of Newton, to reject the distant and detached clock-maker who passed for God with many of his contemporaries. Instead he rediscovered for himself the mysterious and suddenly present God who spoke to Moses from the burning bush, the mysterious and all-sustaining Word made flesh at Bethlehem, and the life-giving Holy Spirit through whom the imaginations of poets are kindled.
>
> p. 146

Guite argues that Coleridge articulates his mature understanding of the "inner and outer," or "primary and secondary" imagination in two compact paragraphs in chapter 13 of the *Biographia Literaria* (pp. 166–177). Coleridge writes:

> The primary IMAGINATION I hold to be the living Power and prime Agent of all human Perception, as a repetition in the finite mind of the eternal act of creation and the infinite I AM. The secondary Imagination I consider as an echo of the former, co-existing with the conscious will, yet still as identical with the primary in the *kind* of its agency, and differing only in *degree*, and in the *mode* of operation.
>
> quoted by Guite, 2012, pp. 166–167

Coleridge's argument, arising in response to the Enlightenment Project and the growing influence of Kant, is a reassertion of the Augustinian concept of illumination that informs the entire tradition of Christian poetry and meditation on language. This tradition articulates the way natural beauty becomes "a revelation of truth" through "tracing *both* world *and* word back to their single source in the holy Logos, the imagination of God" (p. 177). The

Augustinian tradition provides resources for the restoration of the relationship between reason and imagination. It is in the idea of "illumination" that Augustine finds the key to the connection between reason and imagination, the inner world and the outer world, and the Logos within the one redeemed by grace and the Logos at the center of all reality.

As Lewis began the serious search for the truth of the Christian message, the relationship between reason and imagination was critically important. The poem "Reason" written a few years before Lewis became a Christian serves as evidence both of the struggle between reason and imagination and of the desire for their unification in a larger whole. Guite argues that in the poem the two goddesses, Athene (representing reason) and Demeter (representing the fertile power of imagination), vie for a place of honor within the soul of Lewis. Guite writes, "Lewis is still struggling to become a whole person. He cannot by himself personally reconcile these two inner powers, inner goddesses: his reason and his imagination" (2012, pp. 163–164). Lewis cries out in the poem:

> Oh who will reconcile in me both maid and mother,
> Who make in me a concord of the depth and height?
> Who make imagination's dim exploring touch
> Ever report the same as intellectual sight?
> Then could I truly say, and not deceive,
> Then wholly say, that I BELIEVE.
>
> (Lewis, 1964, p. 81)

Eventually, ". . . the coming of Christ into Lewis' life did effect a reconciliation and integration of his powers of reason and imagination—bearing fruit in the works of scholarship, fiction and poetry which followed on from his conversion" (Guite, 2015, p. 165). This fruitful reconciliation is borne out in the third essay of *The Abolition of Man*. If all human life is reduced to the blind agenda of instinct, then reason loses its power to nature and imagination cannot rise above passion. The blind course taken by one generation determines the weaknesses of the next. As Lewis puts it: ". . . the power of Man to make himself what he pleases means, as we have seen, the power of some men to make other men what *they* please" (Lewis, 2001, p. 59). It is the willful power of the "Conditioners" who determine which aspects of "instinctual man" will be chosen to replace the *Tao* to produce the kind of people they want to produce based upon their own passionate desires (pp. 65–66). Lewis writes:

> At the moment, then, of man's victory over Nature, we find the whole human race subjected to some individual men, and those individuals subjected to that in themselves which is purely "natural"—to their irrational impulses. Nature, untrammeled by values, rules the Conditioners and, through them, all humanity. Man's conquest of Nature turns out, in the moment of its consummation, to be Nature's conquest of Man.
>
> pp. 67–68

It is at this juncture that the role of imagination becomes clear. Within the realm of the Objective Moral Law lies the imaginative vision of Reality as a whole. The wise person of old realized that the central problem "had been how to conform the soul to reality, and the solution had been knowledge, self-discipline, and virtue" (p. 77). The teachings and metaphors, objective standards and wisdom narratives of the *Tao* provide the methods, the exemplars, the illumination of the Logos, and the witness of the past to guide the process by which the soul is conformed to Reality—all for the sake of the generations yet to come. When the *Tao* is rejected and the Conditioners exercise their control, all their power is employed to try to "subdue reality to the wishes of men" (p. 77). But this is doomed to failure because "every conquest over Nature increases her domain" (p. 71), and "Man's final conquest [of nature] has proved to be the abolition of Man" (p. 64). Only a new "Natural Philosophy" can offer hope. Only as imagination is reconnected with reason can one begin to "wholly say, I BELIEVE" (Lewis, 1964, p. 81).

This insight can be illustrated in many aspects of the novel. Although there were stirrings of something new in Mark, while he allowed the beauty of Cure Hardy to affect him, his passion to belong, to be in the "inner ring" of N.I.C.E. continues to drive him toward an increased role in their project. He even subverts his own training in intellectual virtue by writing accounts of events before they occurred (Lewis, 2003, pp. 128–132).

As he moves toward the leadership circle, Mark learns from Filostrato that the real goal of man's power over nature is a world without the organic. Trees made of aluminum, "art birds" singing artificially produced bird songs, a planet devoid of organic life, and Mind without bodies. Such a world would be marked by the absence of "birth and breeding and death" (pp. 170–171). The growing ability of men to regulate birth, circumvent sex, and produce the "New Man, the man who will not die, the artificial man, free from Nature" (pp. 172–174) is the real goal of N.I.C.E. That "New Man" is the "Head." One "Man" and not mankind, one "Man" on the throne and not all men, is the real meaning of the power of "Man" over Nature. As Filostrato says, ". . . Man's power over Nature means the power of some men over other men with Nature as the instrument" (p. 175; see also Lewis, 2001, pp. 67–68). Mark, confused and shaken by fear, is taken to see the "Head" who is kept alive by a pseudo-scientific apparatus and the power of the "Macrobes," a life-form greater and more powerful than man. Mark's reaction to the encounter is far different than Jane's reaction to her meeting with the Director. Mark fell and hit his head. But much more happened to him. He realized the threat to life, his life and all life, represented by the Head artificially kept "alive" and he knew he must do "something about Jane." He "must get her, to save his life" (p. 182). Despite his fear, Mark is unable to summon the will to escape N.I.C.E.

After an aborted attempt to escape on his own and a N.I.C.E.-engineered murder charge against him, Mark's "conditioning" makes another leap when he is placed in a room that was ill-proportioned and decorated to produce disorientation (pp. 194–195). It was called the "Objective Room" (p. 331). Mark's reaction was to vaguely realize that:

> Something else—something he vaguely called the "Normal"—apparently existed. He had never thought about it before. But there it was—solid, massive, with a shape of its own, almost like something you could touch, or eat, or fall in love with. It was all mixed up with Jane and fried eggs and soap and sunlight and the rooks cawing at Cure Hardy and the thought that, somewhere outside, daylight was going on at the moment. He was not thinking in moral terms at all; or else (what is much the same thing) he was having his first deeply moral experience. He was choosing a side: the Normal.
>
> p. 297

Subsequent periods of time in the "Objective Room" only served to confirm in Mark, little by little, the idea of normal reality outside of his self-consciousness, outside of his academic discipline, outside of N.I.C.E., and outside of common experience to which or to whom he owes some allegiance. Each hour in the Objective Room strengthened this commitment to "the Normal." As his "conditioning" reached a climax, Mark was asked to trample on a large crucifix. He resisted but Professor Frost continued to say (ironically), "Pray make haste." Mark began to understand that it was "a cross." Mark began "thinking, thinking hard:" "… he turned to Frost and said, 'It's all bloody nonsense, and I'm damned if I do any such thing'" (pp. 253–254).

Mark's reason finally began to think and think hard about the entire conflict between the Normal or Straight and the Crooked, between a vision of someone dying for another and the rejection of life itself. At this moment, Mark begins to make the connection between reason and imagination. His reason is beginning to be illuminated by a deeper and broader possible range of meaning.

Conclusion

I argued in this chapter that *The Abolition of Man* is organized around three significant consequences of the Enlightenment Project. The impact of the Project on Western civilization results in the severing of: fact and value; truth and meaning; and reason and imagination. In addition, these themes are expressed in a variety of ways in the imagery, characters, and action of *That Hideous Strength.* But my analysis would be incomplete if I did not seek to demonstrate that the imaginative climax of the novel is also an effort to point to the reunification of these themes in a robust Trinitarian context.

In the conclusion of *The Abolition of Man*, Lewis suggests that a "new Natural Philosophy" can be imagined (2001, pp. 67–68). The word "imagined" is important. As stated above, imagination is the organ of meaning on which the reason works to determine truth. A new natural philosophy would be one in which the "whole" would not be reduced to the parts. It would attend to the task of analysis with a constant awareness of the relational character of persons in community and in relationship with the "Thou." It would reconnect conscience shaped by the *Tao* to the pursuit of knowledge in order to resist any assertion that human life is driven only by Instinct. It would question the assumption that life is an "infinite unilinear progression" unaltered by the unique or *sui generis*. In other words, Lewis is calling for the reunification of fact and value, truth and meaning, and reason and imagination.

In the concluding scenes of *That Hideous Strength*, Lewis provides a comic and cosmic vision of both the consequences of the death of knowledge and the celebration of the restoration of knowledge. The comic and extravagant banquet scene is an apocalyptic vision of the consequences of severing fact and value, truth and meaning, and reason and imagination. It is a hilarious vision of the consequences of the abandonment of the belief "in knowledge itself" (Lewis, 2003, p. 350). Initially, only the speech by Jules is incoherent. The narrator's account is a savagely satirical riff on the worst possible academic drivel. But, the speech quickly veers from a merely misused word or strained metaphor to utter nonsense. When Wither forces Jules to sit down and tries to reassert order, he utters incoherent nonsense, and chaos and mayhem erupt (p. 342–343). Murder, terror, destruction, rampaging wild beasts, and fire eventually engulfed the entire N.I.C.E. complex. In this extravagant exaggerated scene, Lewis provides a comic yet terrifying vision of the consequences of the modern project. Modernity leads to the "curse of Babel: They that have despised the word of God, from them shall the word of man also be taken away" (p. 348).

A very different banquet is simultaneously occurring at St. Anne's-on-the-Hill. The women of St. Anne's are clothed in elegant dresses chosen by each other from the array of options in the Wardrobe. The men have prepared the meal and are dressed in formal attire. It is a banquet characterized by love, by beauty, by the infusion of the vitality of life, and by the symbolic intersection of the natural and the supernatural. Instead of N.I.C.E., with its closed ideology of materialistic naturalism, whose ultimate goal is the eradication of life, the community of St. Anne's celebrates an open universe in which the natural is completed in the supernatural. The joy and vitality mythically attributed to a midsummer night fills the air. The sacred order represented by Venus has descended upon St. Anne's and all of nature celebrates. Ransom, the Pendragon and Christ figure of the Trilogy, is preparing to return to Perelandra (Venus) and is pronouncing the blessing of God on each one present. The atmosphere is crackling with wonder and joy and a kind of deliciousness and freshness that "seemed to be blowing into the room" (p. 374). In this setting, Lewis seems to be suggesting the context for a new, non-reductive natural philosophy that celebrates the gift of life and joyfully affirms the One whose creativity bequeaths all with life and significance in the long history of His redemptive plan. And by so doing, the Triune God invites us to join the cosmic dance.

The connections between *The Abolition of Man* and *That Hideous Strength* are many and varied. I have only suggested a few in this chapter. The analysis of the contemporary situation offered by Lewis in *The Abolition of Man* is brought to life in the creative climax of the Ransom trilogy. Lewis could say: I BELIEVE. He did argue that fact and value, truth and meaning, and reason and imagination must be held together, and are being held together, by the Logos that illumines all Reality.

Works cited

Aristotle (2002), *Nicomachean Ethics* (trans. J. Sachs). Newburyport, MA: Focus Publishing.

Book of Common Prayer (1559). Online. https://www.wwnorton.com/college/english/nael/ 17century/topic_1/matrimon.htm [accessed May 11, 2016].

Guite, M. (2012), *Faith, Hope and Poetry: Theology and the Poetic Imagination.* Farnham: Ashgate Publishing.

Guite, M. (2015), "Lewis and the feminine voice in poetry," in C. Curtis and M.P. Key (eds.) *Women and C. S. Lewis: What his Life and Literature Reveal for Today's Culture*. Oxford: Lion Hudson, pp. 159–166.

Hilder, M.B. (2013), *The Gender Dance: Ironic Subversion in C.S. Lewis' Cosmic Trilogy.* New York: Peter Lang.

Kant, I. (1952), *Critique of Judgement* (trans. J.C. Meredith). Great Books of the Western World, Vol. 42. Chicago, IL: Encyclopaedia Britannica.

Lewis, C.S. (1964), "Reason," in *Poems* (ed. W. Hooper). New York: Harcourt Brace and Company.

Lewis, C.S. (1969), "Bluspels and Flalansferes: A Semantic Nightmare," in *Selected Literary Essays* (ed. W. Hooper). Cambridge: Cambridge University Press.

Lewis, C.S. (2001), *The Abolition of Man.* New York: HarperCollins.

Lewis, C.S. (2003), *That Hideous Strength*. New York: Scribner.

Nagel, T. (2012), *Mind and Cosmos: Why the Materialist Neo-Darwinian Conception of Nature is Almost Certainly False*. Oxford: Oxford University Press.

Oxford English Dictionary (1989), 2nd edition, Vols. I–XIX. Oxford: Clarendon Press.

Index

www.ingramcontent.com/pod-product-compliance
Ingram Content Group UK Ltd.
Pitfield, Milton Keynes, MK11 3LW, UK
UKHW020144290926
15471UKWH00004B/690

9 781350 082236